Do Your Own Conveyancing

About the author

Paul Butt, LLB, is a solicitor and a principal lecturer at the College of Law, Chester. He is the author of several books, on landlord and tenant issues (including *Renting and Letting* with Peter Wilde), conveyancing and other property matters, and a lecturer to the profession.

Do Your Own Conveyancing

Paul Butt

 CONSUMERS' ASSOCIATION

Which? Books are commissioned by
Consumers' Association and published by
Which? Ltd, 2 Marylebone Road, London NW1 4DF
Email: books@which.net

Distributed by The Penguin Group:
Penguin Books Ltd, 80 Strand, London WC2R 0RL

First edition February 2000
Second edition June 2004
Copyright © 2000, 2004 Which? Ltd

The Standard Conditions of Sale in Appendix II are printed with permission from Oyez and
the Law Society

British Library Cataloguing in Publication Data
A catalogue record for *Do Your Own Conveyancing* is available from the British Library

ISBN 0 85202 992 6

For a full list of *Which?* books, please call 0800 252 100, access our website at
www.which.net or write to Which? Books, Freepost, Hertford SG14 1SH.

Original cover design by Sarah Harmer
Cover photograph by gettyimages

Typeset by Saxon Graphics Ltd, Derby
Printed and bound in Wales by Creative Print and Design

Contents

★ An asterisk next to the name of an organisation in the text indicates that the address can be found in this section.

Introduction

Despite the fact that an estimated 1.5 million households in England and Wales move home each year the procedure for buying and selling houses remains old-fashioned, slow and cumbersome and can involve a considerable amount of time, money and stress for both buyer and seller. Even when you use professionals, whose fees can be very high, it is not unusual to find yourself doing most of the chasing and running around.

Government proposals for Home Information Packs and for conveyancing to be carried out electronically over the Internet – both of which it is hoped will speed up the process – are still some years from fruition. So, in the meantime, being in control of the whole process is a tempting option. This book shows you that, although the legal process can seem daunting, most house sales and purchases are straightforward, and with time, care and the right guidance it is perfectly possible for you to handle your own legal work on an uncomplicated sale or purchase.

There are some circumstances, however, when the work must be left to the experts, or where professional advice will be necessary before proceeding, and the book highlights these.

Selling and buying a house: the process at a glance

- Seller places house on market

- Buyer and seller informally agree sale; there is no legally binding contract at this stage

- Seller sends pre-contract package to buyer. This contains the terms on which the seller is prepared to sell, proof of the seller's ownership and other information about the house

---

- Buyer studies the pre-contract package and makes various searches and enquiries about the house, e.g. to ensure that there are no adverse rights which will affect the buyer's ownership

- Buyer ensures that the finance is available with which to buy the house

- Buyer and seller exchange contracts. Buyer pays a deposit of 5–10 per cent of the price as a sign of good faith. Both are now legally committed to the transaction

- Buyer prepares the transfer (the document which will transfer ownership from the seller) and sends it to the seller for approval

- Buyer asks the seller for details of the arrangements for completion

- Seller approves the transfer and arrangements for completion are finalised

- The transfer is signed by buyer and seller and retained by the seller until completion

- Buyer makes final searches at Land Registry

- Completion takes place – the buyer hands over the balance of the money and receives the keys and the transfer in return

- Buyer pays any stamp duty land tax that is due and registers the purchase at Land Registry to become legal owner

Chapter 1

Why do your own conveyancing?

Most of us have been through it at least once, many of us on far too many occasions – the hassle, strain, toil and stress of moving house. Looking for a new house and trying to find a buyer for one you wish to sell are taxing enough, but once you have taken these first steps things all too often seem to go from bad to worse.

And so the nightmare begins. Negotiating with estate agents and surveyors, taking time off work to see conveyancers, and constantly phoning them all to find out what is happening.

Buying a house is recognised as one of the most stressful situations a person will experience throughout his or her life. However, having more control over the situation, perhaps doing the legal work yourself and not having to rely on others, can help to make the process more bearable, and this book provides information and guidance to help you do this.

Problems with conveyancers

Problems with conveyancers, that is, solicitors and licensed conveyancers, usually arise for one of two reasons. The first is the legal system itself. The procedure for buying and selling houses in England and Wales is old-fashioned, slow and cumbersome. Changes are going to be made (see page 21 for the government's plans), but it will be some years yet before these are fully implemented.

Conveyancers are often unfairly blamed for these faults in the system, for example gazumping, a situation in which a seller accepts a higher offer from another buyer at a late stage in the transaction (see page 19). Under the present system, if a seller has agreed a sale price with a buyer and is waiting for the legal work to be completed before a legally binding contract is entered into, and another buyer offers a higher price, the seller is not legally obliged to sell to the first buyer.

Unfortunately, conveyancers are often themselves at fault, and horror stories abound of conveyancers who are too slow, charge too much, or who fail to get the money through on time for completion to take place when agreed, of buyers setting off down the motorway with their furniture, not sure if they will have a house to move into at the other end, or even having to spend the night in removal vans with their furniture. The main complaints, however, are regarding delay and lack of information. Doing your own conveyancing means that you know exactly what stage the transaction has reached.

Traditionally, conveyancers are instructed only once a buyer for a house has been found. The seller's conveyancer then has to collect together a variety of information and draft the contract for sale for inclusion in the pre-contract package to send to the buyer. This in itself can delay matters for a week or more, but by doing your own conveyancing you can make sure that the pre-contract package is ready before a buyer is found, so that it can be sent off on the day any sale is agreed. The government's plans for a Home Information Pack (see page 21) will make it compulsory for all this information to be in place before a house is put on the market.

Although conveyancers are sometimes slow and expensive, they usually carry out the work competently. However, increasing competition for business has resulted in conveyancers now quoting lower fees for conveyancing, and claims have been made that this has sometimes resulted in a poorer quality of work being provided. There has been much discussion within the profession as to whether conveyancers offering cut-price conveyancing incur a higher than usual number of claims for negligence. Whatever the answer, the old adage that 'you get what you pay for' normally holds good.

Of course, when you are doing your own conveyancing, buying or selling your own house, you will take extra special care that everything is 100 per cent correct – the 'client' would expect nothing less!

Will I save any money by doing my own conveyancing?

Another reason for doing the conveyancing yourself might be to save money, to save the fees you would otherwise have had to pay a conveyancer. How much you will save largely depends upon the nature of the transaction itself, and the value of the property.

There is no set scale of charges for conveyancing work. Fees for a sale or purchase will differ from firm to firm, and from region to region (for example, fees in London and the South East of England may be somewhat higher), as each firm will have different overheads and charging policies. They can range from quotes of around £350 each for a sale or purchase, and perhaps £600 upwards for a sale and purchase, depending upon the purchase price, and are exclusive of VAT at the standard rate of 17.5 per cent. However, these are very much minimum fees, and many firms will quote much higher. Remember that in general you do get what you pay for, so a firm quoting a higher fee may provide a better service. Remember also that these are just the conveyancer's fees. In addition, on a purchase, you will have to pay for all the various outgoings, search fees, Land Registry fees and the like. There may also be a considerable sum in stamp duty land tax to pay. These will amount to several hundred pounds more and will be incurred whoever does the conveyancing.

Lender's conveyancer's fees

A complication arises when you are buying the house with the aid of a mortgage loan from a bank or building society. The lender will require a conveyancer to act on its behalf in connection with the loan. Normally, the lender will instruct the conveyancer acting for you, as this saves everyone involved time and money. The fees quoted above for acting for the buyer will normally also cover acting for the lender. If you are doing your own conveyancing, the lender will still require a conveyancer to act on its behalf as one of the terms of the loan, and will expect you to pay that conveyancer's costs.

How much should you expect to pay a conveyancer for acting for the lender when you are doing your own conveyancing?

Unfortunately, the amount of work to be done for a lender is much the same as that done by a conveyancer acting for a buyer. When the conveyancer is acting for both lender and buyer the work is done only once on behalf of both clients; when acting just for the lender, the conveyancer will still carry out the same checks and so on as when acting for the buyer as well. Although you will have done this work yourself, the lender's conveyancer will still need to redo it on behalf of the lender. The conveyancer cannot rely on the work carried out by you – for example, you might be planning to pocket the mortgage advance and disappear – and, of course, he or she will need to check that you have done the work correctly.

It is therefore likely that conveyancers' quotes for acting solely on behalf of the lender will only be a little (if any) less than those for acting for you as well, so if you make any savings at all here they will be small. If you are buying with the aid of a mortgage loan, it is therefore definitely not worth doing your own conveyancing if all you are concerned with is saving money.

Similarly, if you are selling a house which is subject to a mortgage, the lender will require a conveyancer to be instructed to protect its interests and you will pay the fees. The work involved here would normally have been included in the fees of the conveyancer acting for you on a sale, but where you are doing your own conveyancing will have to be paid for separately. Fees are usually in the region of between £150 and £250, plus VAT.

Other expenses

Whether you do your own conveyancing or instruct a conveyancer, there are various other expenses you will have to meet in connection with the legal work. These additional expenses, or 'disbursements', are always charged extra, over and above the conveyancer's quoted fee for time spent carrying out the work.

Disbursements include stamp duty land tax (a government tax which can amount to several thousands of pounds, depending upon the value of the property), Land Registry fees (for registering the transaction), and fees for making 'searches', that is, obtaining information about the property from various public and other bodies (see pages 105–9). Search and Land Registry fees will amount to a minimum of £200, depending upon the nature and value of the property.

All the above fees are payable whether you do your own conveyancing or a conveyancer does it for you, and cannot be avoided. However, they should be payable only once if you do your own conveyancing and a conveyancer acts for the lender – there should be no need for the lender's conveyancer to repeat the searches you have made, though he or she will need to consider the information revealed by those searches in the same way as you will.

Satisfaction

Perhaps more than saving money, you will have the satisfaction that comes with any do-it-yourself work. There will be a real sense of achievement in having mastered a new skill, and knowing a lot more about your new house because you have studied all the legal documentation, seen all the searches and enquiries and so on, could even enhance your enjoyment of it once you move in.

DIY conveyancing

No law says that you cannot do your own conveyancing when buying or selling a property (although there are restrictions on unqualified persons doing conveyancing work for other people). The mechanics of most conveyancing transactions are quite straightforward, so provided you take care and follow the guidance given in this book, you should be able to tackle the sale or purchase of a house with confidence. However, there are certain types of transaction which an unqualified person should not attempt (see below), and occasionally problems arise for which you will need to take immediate legal advice.

Even if you decide not to do it yourself, you will find the information in this book useful in understanding just what is involved in buying or selling a house and the work that your conveyancer must complete before you can move.

How many hours will it take?

You should be able to tackle a sale or a purchase in about 12 to 15 hours, depending upon the particular circumstances of the transaction – and your word-processing skills – and doing your own conveyancing is not too onerous a job for most people to contemplate. The work will be spread over the period of the transaction, perhaps an hour or two per week. Although this does not seem very long, you must remember that you will still have to do all the hundreds of other things that need arranging when you are moving house, and that often a swift reply (preferably the same day) to any queries will be required to avoid delaying the transaction.

What will I need in order to do my own conveyancing?

Apart from time (see above), you will need the following:

- various forms (see page 47 for the forms required when selling a house, and page 89 for those required for a purchase)
- a word processor or typewriter
- access to a photocopying machine. Most copies that you will require will be second copies of documents you are typing yourself, so if you are using a word processor you can simply print out an extra copy. However, documents you obtain from elsewhere will also need to be copied, and many local shops, petrol stations and so on offer photocopying at reasonable rates. It is a good idea to plan ahead – find out beforehand where you can get your copies done as once you get started you might not have the time to go running round trying to find somewhere
- access to a phone during the day – there are various matters that will need to be sorted out over the telephone in order to save time and it will be very difficult to ensure a speedy completion if you cannot make (and receive) phone calls during the day
- access to a fax machine – again, this is particularly useful in order to save time and reduce the risk of delaying the process
- access to the Internet – this is not essential, but many of the forms you will need can be downloaded free of charge from here
- patience.

When not to do it yourself

If you follow carefully the guidance given in this book you will be able to deal with all the legal matters arising with an ordinary house purchase. However, you must be careful. Certain problems, if they occur, will require you to take legal advice from a conveyancer and these are highlighted throughout the book. If a problem arises that is not covered by this book and you are unsure, you must ask a conveyancer for help. If you do not take advice, you risk ending up with a house that you can never sell, or losing all the money you are paying for it. At the very least, you risk paying out substantial damages for breach of contract. There will usually be two conveyancers involved in the transaction – one acting for the seller, the other for your lender. The seller's conveyancer cannot advise you, but you can ask him or her to explain any letters sent which you do not understand.

The lender's conveyancer may be more helpful; like you, he or she will want to ensure everything is in order before risking the lender's money in buying the house. If a problem arises, you will in any event have to ask whether the situation is acceptable to the lender, and if not what remedial steps you are required to take. So the lender's conveyancer may well be your obvious choice for advice. However, you cannot expect to be phoning the lender's conveyancer every five minutes for free advice. Doing it yourself means just that.

Situations where the complications arising are likely to be beyond the abilities of someone who is undertaking their own conveyancing are listed below.

Property outside England and Wales
The advice given in this book is applicable only to properties in England and Wales. Scotland, Northern Ireland, the Isle of Man and other countries have their own systems of conveyancing and you must consult a conveyancer qualified in the law of the country concerned when buying or selling property outside England and Wales.

Unregistered property
The ownership of most houses in England and Wales is 'registered' at Land Registry (see Appendix I). The Registry keeps detailed records of who owns the land and many of the rights and obligations affecting the owner. However, some land has still not been placed on the Register and a different system of conveyancing from

that outlined in this book applies. If you discover that the land you are buying or selling is unregistered, ask a conveyancer to deal with the matter for you.

Leasehold houses

Although most houses are freehold, there are some parts of England and Wales where houses are sometimes owned on a long lease. The law here is more complicated and should not be tackled by a beginner.

Flats

Most flats will be held on leases, although occasionally they are freehold. Either way, the law is too complicated for a beginner to deal with either the sale or the purchase.

Buying or selling at an auction

Again, more complicated legal considerations apply to an auction sale and these should be undertaken only by someone who is legally qualified. In particular, beware if buying at an auction; the normal rule that a contract for the purchase of land is not legally enforceable unless it is in writing does not apply in the case of an auction sale. If you are the highest bidder at an auction and the property is knocked down to you, then that is a binding contract and you are committed to buy; there is no pre-contract 'cooling off' period during which you can change your mind.

Buying part of a house or a plot of land

There are special considerations when part of a house or garden is being bought or sold, so such transactions should be dealt with by a conveyancer.

Buying or selling where part of the house is occupied by a tenant

There are legal complications here which require the use of a conveyancer.

Buying from a local authority or housing association under right-to-buy

Special rules of law apply to this situation which are outside the scope of this book.

Buying when there is a 'shared ownership' transaction with a housing association

Special rules of law again mean that this kind of transaction should be left to a qualified person.

Buying or selling on divorce or separation

Buying or selling in these circumstances requires specialist knowledge of matrimonial law as well as conveyancing, and so should be avoided by anyone unqualified in both these matters.

Buying or selling property with a commercial use

This book is only concerned with the sale and purchase of **residential property**. If the property is used for commercial purposes, or you are buying property with the intention of using it for commercial purposes, for example a shop, then you will not be able to do your own conveyancing. This will be the case even if the property is also used for residential purposes, for example there is living accommodation at the rear of or above the shop.

Buying or selling when a limited company is involved

If you are buying from a limited company, or wish to buy your house in the name of a company that you control, you will need professional advice, as detailed aspects of company law may be involved.

Buying from a builder or developer

The documentation used in a sale by a builder or developer will be different from that explained in this book. Various other problems can arise which mean that you need to instruct a conveyancer to act for you.

Contract races

In a contract race, the seller is dealing with two (or more) potential buyers who are in a 'race' to buy the house. The idea is that the first one able to exchange contracts will win the race and buy the house. Whether acting for yourself or using a conveyancer, avoid contract races at all costs, unless you are really desperate to buy. You run the risk of incurring considerable expense on surveys, search fees and so on, only to find that you are pipped at the post and someone else buys the house. Contract races are not for the beginner.

Other situations where problems are likely

In addition to the situations above where you should definitely not act for yourself, there are circumstances in which you need to consider very carefully whether to do it yourself. The following situations are where problems are very likely and you must be in a position to devote more time and care to the transaction.

Buying and selling

When selling your house and buying another at the same time, you will of course be taking on twice the amount of work. Will you be able to afford the time? You will also have to ensure that you manage both transactions so that they proceed in unison. You will need to ensure that you exchange contracts on both sale and purchase on the same day and that completion is also set for the same day. If this is your first time at doing it yourself, think very carefully about taking on a sale *and* purchase. Although possible, it is not easy, and even conveyancers sometimes have problems co-ordinating the two transactions.

Chain transactions

One of the main reasons for delays and problems in conveyancing transactions is the chain. This arises when A is buying from B, who in turn is buying from C, who is then buying from D, and so on. If you are doing your own conveyancing, it may be difficult to contact you at short notice and your inability to exchange contracts over the phone to speed things up will delay matters. If there is a long chain involved, think very carefully about continuing to go it alone, particularly if you are buying and selling at the same time.

Dealing with an unlicensed conveyancer on the other side

In theory, there is no reason why both buyer and seller should not do their own conveyancing. However, if the person you are dealing with is also doing his or her own conveyancing, you will need to be extra careful as the likelihood of problems arising is increased. Remember, he or she may not be as careful as you will be.

Being prepared

Once you have decided upon doing it yourself, what do you do next? First, read all the way through this book to get a feel of what is involved. Next, before putting your house on the market (in the case of a sale), or deciding on a new house (in the case of a purchase), read carefully again the parts of the book dealing with selling or buying, whichever is relevant to your situation.

Only when you have got to grips with what is involved in the conveyancing process should you put your house on the market or decide on a new house. 'Be prepared' should be your motto. Once the conveyancing procedure is under way it is like a roller coaster; you cannot stop halfway through and keep checking on what comes next – any delay could be seriously detrimental to the success of the transaction. You need to anticipate and be ready for the next stage of the transaction.

Gazumping and gazundering – can they be avoided?

Gazumping

Gazumping is a problem when house prices are increasing rapidly. It is a particular problem in London and the South East of England. The act of gazumping came to the fore in the property boom of the late 1980s, when people were so keen to get into the market that they were prepared to pay ridiculous prices for property, and many sellers used the system to overturn previously agreed deals.

Even when a buyer and seller 'agree' a price for a house, this agreement is not legally binding until written contracts are exchanged, perhaps six to eight weeks later. During this time, the house remains on the market and estate agents will still show around prospective buyers. This is to protect against the possibility of the original buyer backing out at the last minute, which results in the seller, after wasting several weeks, having to start marketing the house once again.

However, in a market where prices are rising rapidly, there is a danger that the seller will decide to accept a higher offer, and this often occurs just before the original buyer is about to exchange. At this stage, the original buyer has incurred expenses in surveys, searches and other legal fees, is planning to move in a few weeks' time, and then discovers the seller is going to sell to someone else at a higher price. The original buyer has been gazumped.

When gazumping occurs, the original buyer is sometimes given the opportunity of making an increased offer for the house, although often he or she is just informed that the seller has accepted a higher offer and that the sale is off.

It is the long delay between the parties informally agreeing the sale and the sale becoming legally binding that allows gazumping to happen, and anything you can do to reduce this delay will lessen the opportunity for it to happen. You can, for example:

- arrange your loan in principle before finding a house
- be ready to start the conveyancing work the day you agree to buy, for example by making sure that you have all the relevant forms in advance
- make your pre-contract searches as soon as you agree to buy. By doing it yourself, you will be able to make the searches days earlier than if you have to make an appointment to see a conveyancer to act for you and then wait for him or her to do them for you.

However, the delay cannot be avoided altogether and while there is this delay, there is always the risk of the seller accepting a better offer.

Lockout agreements

The only way of preventing gazumping is to get the seller to enter into a legally binding agreement not to sell the property to anyone else during a specified period of time, which should be long enough to allow you as buyer to undertake all the work required before you can safely enter into a binding contract to purchase. This agreement is known as a 'lockout agreement'.

The snag with lockout agreements is that although the seller is prevented from selling elsewhere, there is nothing to stop you as buyer changing your mind and deciding not to buy after all. It is therefore somewhat one-sided, and the seller might take the view that it is unfair for you to expect him or her to agree to wait for you for, say, a month, and then find that you do not want the house after all. In times where the market is rising (where prices are increasing rapidly), the seller might be reluctant to agree to being locked into your deal and losing the opportunity of selling to someone else at a higher price. So lockout agreements are not much used in practice, particularly where there is a seller's market.

Gazundering

Gazundering is the equivalent of gazumping in a market where house prices are falling. The buyer and seller agree a price and then, just when the seller was expecting to exchange, the buyer states that he or she will only exchange if the seller agrees to a reduced price. Again, the long delay between agreeing a sale and exchange allows this practice to continue. A seller can take steps to reduce the risk of this by preparing a Home Information Pack in advance of putting the house on the market (see page 21). This will reduce the delay prior to exchange and thus the risk of gazundering.

Insurance
It is possible to obtain insurance to cover you for the wasted expenditure should gazumping or gazundering happen to you. Such policies will often also cover you for wasted costs should the transaction fall through for other reasons, for example problems with the seller's ownership status. The premiums for such insurance are quite low. Such policies are offered by some lenders, but are also available independently of a lender.

Government review of conveyancing

The present government, concerned about the reappearance of gazumping, set up a working party to look into the conveyancing procedure to determine whether it could be reformed and gazumping prevented altogether. The consultation paper was published in December 1998. However, research revealed that gazumping only occurred in a very small number of cases, about 2 per cent, although the wasted expense caused when it did occur was found to be great.

The Scottish system (in which contracts become legally binding as soon as a verbal agreement is reached) was considered and rejected. Instead, proposals were put forward that centred on reducing the delay before contracts could be exchanged. These included the seller providing a more comprehensive pre-contract package (a Home Information Pack – or Seller's Pack, as it was originally called) containing all the information a buyer now has to obtain before he or she can exchange, as well as a form of survey of the house. Much controversy surrounded the inclusion of the survey, as it would cost the seller, who presently does not incur the survey costs, up to £500 in every case. It has been announced that the Home Information Pack will not become compulsory until 1 January 2007.

The government also intends that eventually it will be possible to carry out all of the stages in a conveyancing transaction electronically over the Internet. The Land Registration Act 2002 (in force as from 13 October 2003) lays the legislative foundation for this, but again it is unlikely that a pilot scheme will be introduced before 2006, and it will be several years after that before it will become compulsory. When the scheme is introduced, special provisions will be introduced to allow for do-it-yourself conveyancing.

Chapter 2

An overview of selling and buying a house

'Conveyancing' is the name given to the process of transferring the ownership of a house or land. The buyer needs to ensure that he or she gets good 'title' to the land, that the person selling the house actually has the right to sell it. The ownership of land often carries with it other benefits and burdens. So, for example, a house might need the benefit of a right of way over adjoining land (that is, the right to walk, or drive, across that other land) in order to gain access to it. The conveyancer must check that such a right is in existence. The house may also be subject to a covenant, such as the obligation not to use the land other than for a specified purpose, or to a right of way in favour of a neighbour. The conveyancer needs to check to ascertain whether there are any such burdens affecting the land.

The system of conveyancing is designed to ensure that the buyer gets the land together with all the rights that go with it, and knows about any restrictions in advance. Other pitfalls that should be resolved through the conveyancing process include the seller becoming bankrupt, disputes over boundaries and fences, and even members of a family refusing to move out on the day fixed for completion.

A typical conveyancing transaction, whether a sale or purchase, contains two major 'landmarks', which are exchange of contracts and completion, plus the three stages: before contract, before completion and after completion. Each of these is described below and over the following pages.

What happens at each stage will depend upon whether you are buying or selling. Although this book looks at buying and selling separately, much of the process is the same for both.

What is involved in selling a house?

Before contract

The first step towards selling a house is finding a buyer, either with the help of an estate agent or perhaps by advertising it yourself. Remember that when you agree to sell to a buyer at a particular price, this agreement is not legally binding; the buyer or seller can change his or her mind without the risk of any comeback or having to pay any penalties. (It is this rule that enables the practices of gazumping and gazundering to flourish – see page 19.) A contract for the sale of land is only legally binding when it is in writing and signed by both parties, and at this early stage it will be some weeks before either party can safely enter into a binding contract.

Warning

Never try to hurry things along by persuading a prospective buyer to agree in writing to buy at this stage. The rule that there is no binding agreement until exchange is there to protect both buyer and seller and it could well be to your own disadvantage to do this. In any event, if it came to court a judge may decide that this rule is so well established that you cannot get round it in this way.

Assuming that you have a buyer and have agreed a price, the next thing you must do as seller is to prepare a 'pre-contract package' containing a variety of information about the property, including proof of the seller's ownership and details of rights others may have over the land, for example easements or covenants. The pre-contract package will also contain the contract setting out the terms on which the seller is prepared to sell the house. You can save time here if you prepare the package as soon as you put the house on the market. The requirement for a Home Information Pack is not due to come into force until 1 January 2007, but there is no reason why you should not include in your pre-contract package all the information and searches that a buyer would otherwise need to obtain.

The pre-contract package is then sent to the buyer, who will consider all the information and the terms of the contract and decide whether he or she is prepared to enter into a legally binding contract. The buyer may wish to ask you a few more questions about the property or your ownership of it, or may wish to renegotiate some of the terms of the contract. He or she will also be making various searches, that is, finding out as much information as possible from public records, for example those held by the local authority.

The buyer will also need to ensure that he or she has the money available to buy. This normally entails waiting for a formal offer of a mortgage loan from a bank or building society. The buyer will also have to ensure that sufficient funds are available to pay the deposit, which can be up to 10 per cent of the purchase price, that is usually required on exchange.

The pre-contract stage is the longest part of the transaction and usually takes six weeks or more. It is common for sellers to instruct conveyancers only when a buyer has been found. The conveyancer then has to gather all the information and prepare the pre-contract package, which can easily delay matters for a couple of weeks. However, this can be reduced if you have your pre-contract package already prepared when the buyer is found so that it can be sent off to the buyer or his or her conveyancer immediately. If you include all the searches the buyer would otherwise need to make, this will further help to speed things up. Doing it yourself can therefore save you time, even if it does not save you much money!

Exchange of contracts

When the buyer has made all the necessary enquiries and is satisfied with the results, and has also made the necessary financial arrangements, the parties can safely enter into a legally binding contract. However, first of all they will have to agree on a completion date, that is, the date when the buyer will hand over the balance of the money and will be entitled to move in. Completion will normally be fixed for a couple of weeks after exchange.

A legally binding contract is entered into by 'exchange of contracts'. Two identical copies of the contract are prepared; the seller signs one and the buyer the other. But the contract only becomes binding when the two original copies are 'exchanged', that is, the buyer gives his or her signed copy to the seller, and the seller likewise gives the copy he or she has signed to the buyer. Should either party subsequently allege a breach of contract and commence court proceedings, the court would request proof that the contract exists, and either party will therefore have no difficulty in proving that the other entered into the contract. (Note that courts generally insist on originals, so supplying a photocopy of the contract in any court proceedings will usually be inadequate for the purpose.)

On exchange, the buyer and seller are both legally bound to go through with the transaction. Should either of them wish to withdraw (without a good legal reason), he or she will be in breach of contract and liable to the other for substantial damages for any loss suffered. The deposit handed over by the buyer to the seller on exchange (traditionally 10 per cent of the purchase price, although nowadays a smaller sum is often paid) acts as part payment (that is, the buyer only has to pay the balance of the purchase price on completion), but more importantly it acts as a guarantee that the buyer will go through with the transaction. If the buyer refuses to go ahead with the purchase once contracts have been exchanged, the seller is entitled to keep the deposit even if he or she suffers no financial loss. Only in exceptional circumstances will a buyer be able to withdraw from the transaction without losing the deposit.

There is no similar guarantee to the buyer that the seller will not withdraw. Of course, if the seller did refuse to go through with the sale for no good legal reason, he or she would be in breach of contract and the buyer would be entitled to sue for damages.

Before completion

Most of the seller's work has now been done. The buyer will draft the 'Transfer', that is, the document which transfers ownership from the seller to the buyer, and this will be sent to the seller for approval. All the seller needs to do is to ensure that the terms of the Transfer agree with the terms of the contract, for example that the price is correctly stated.

The buyer will also ask for details of the arrangements to be made for completion. This will include where completion will take place, arrangements for handing over the keys and for paying off any existing mortgage on the house.

The Transfer will then need to be signed by both parties and retained by the seller ready for completion. The seller must arrange to give vacant possession to the buyer on the day fixed for completion. This means that the house must be empty and suitable for the buyer to move in, for example that no furniture or piles of rubbish are left lying around.

Completion

On the completion date, the buyer will hand over the balance of the money (usually this will be sent by direct transfer between bank accounts) and will receive in return the Transfer, and of course, the keys.

After completion

There is little for the seller to do after completion, except congratulate him- or herself on a job well done!

What is involved in buying a house?

As mentioned earlier, buying a house involves much the same procedure as selling.

Before contract

Before a buyer enters into a binding contract, three areas need to be covered carefully – legal matters, financial matters and insurance.

Legal matters
You will need to ensure that the seller is entitled to sell the house and find out what obligations will be binding on you if you buy it. You will also need to make sure that you will receive all the rights over neighbouring land necessary for you to enjoy the house properly, for example if the drains pass through someone else's land, that you get a legal right for them to do so.

The seller will supply you with a 'pre-contract package' of documents and information about the house. This will include the contract for the sale, which you must check to ensure it is in order, and details of the 'title' to the land. This is proof of the seller's right to sell, together with details of the rights and obligations affecting the land.

However, the seller does not have to supply all the information a buyer needs in order to decide whether to proceed with the transaction, so the buyer will need to make various searches, that is, enquiries of various public bodies, including the local council, to find out as much about the house as possible. If anything untoward is discovered at this stage, remember that you are not legally committed to buy and have no liability to the seller. Equally, the seller can decide not to sell.

Financial matters

You must not enter into a legally binding contract to buy unless and until you are certain that you will be able to afford the purchase. There are two elements here. If you are buying with the aid of a loan, can you really afford the repayments? For example, what would be your position if you (or your partner if you are buying a house jointly) lost your job? Remember, a mortgage is a long-term commitment; you will be borrowing the money over a period of 20 or 25 years. Failure to keep up your repayments can result in you losing your home – if you do not abide by the terms of the loan, the lender can take possession of the house and sell it to recover what is due to it.

You should also consider your finances in the short term. Taking into account all the expenses involved in the transaction, will you have sufficient funds to be able to hand over the full amount of the purchase price on completion? You will need to do your calculations very carefully, particularly if you are relying on the proceeds of the sale of your present house. A simple guide to making these calculations is provided on page 45.

If you will be relying on a loan of any kind, you must not enter into a legally binding contract unless and until you have received (and accepted if required) a formal offer of that loan. Do not rely on verbal assurances that the loan will be forthcoming. You must also check the terms of the loan offer to ensure that the amount that will actually be payable on completion will be sufficient for your needs. Lenders sometimes make deductions or retentions from the loan, for example to cover necessary repairs, so the amount you actually receive from them may be less than you expected.

You also need to be able to pay the deposit that will be required on exchange – this is usually up to 10 per cent of the purchase price. Do you have sufficient savings to pay this? If not, it may be possible to borrow the deposit, or in the case of a sale *and* purchase, to use the deposit paid over to you by your buyer, although this may not always be possible when you are doing your own conveyancing (see page 117).

Insurance

In certain circumstances, depending upon the terms of the contract, the buyer is liable to insure the house as soon as contracts are exchanged. If this is so, you must make sure that you are able to effect that insurance as from the date of exchange.

Exchange of contracts

Once you are satisfied that you can afford the house, and you have discovered all that it is legally necessary to know about it, contracts can then be exchanged if, in the light of that information, you still wish to buy it. A completion date convenient to both buyer and seller will be agreed and both parties will then be bound to proceed with the transaction.

Before completion

The buyer must now draft the document that transfers the ownership to him or her from the seller. This is called the Transfer (see page 122) and is a standard form. Once drafted, it will be sent to the seller for his or her approval. You will also need to enquire of the seller what arrangements are to be made with regard to completion, handing over the keys and so on. Immediately prior to completion a search will have to be made at Land Registry; this is a last-minute check to make sure that no further entries have been made on the Register of title that could adversely affect the ownership of the house. You must also confirm that the funds to be handed over on completion will be available to you on the completion date.

Completion

On completion, you will hand over the balance of the purchase price and receive in return the Transfer signed by the seller transferring the house into your name – together with the keys.

After completion

The buyer's work does not end on completion. You will then have to pay any stamp duty land tax required to the Inland Revenue and submit a form containing details of the transaction. Once you have received confirmation that any existing mortgage has been paid off, you will then need to register the purchase at Land Registry so that your ownership of the house can be confirmed. There are strict time limits (and penalties) within which these steps must be taken.

Warning

This chapter gives only a brief overview of the steps involved in a typical conveyancing transaction. It is intended to provide you with a flavour of what is involved in doing your own conveyancing before you go on to study the precise steps in detail later on in this book, and should not be relied on for guidance in actually carrying out the work. Do not start your own conveyancing unless you are sure that you know what is involved and that you will be able to cope.

Chapter 3

Some background law

An appreciation of some basic law is essential to help you to understand what is happening in the conveyancing transaction. Note, however, that this chapter provides only an introduction to the principles involved. Although these should be sufficient for most ordinary conveyancing transactions, they should not be regarded as a comprehensive statement of the law, and you should seek professional advice if you encounter anything not covered in here.

Ownership of land

The law in England and Wales recognises two forms of ownership of land. These are:

- **freehold**, which gives the right to the land forever; and
- **leasehold**, which gives the right to the land for a fixed period, for example 99 years.

This book is intended to deal with the sale and purchase of **freehold land only**; if you are buying and selling leasehold land, the terms of the lease giving you the right to occupy the land must be considered very carefully and require the advice of a conveyancer.

Rights over land

As well as recognising rights of ownership, the law also recognises rights over land which fall short of ownership. These are sometimes referred to by lawyers as third party rights, that is, the rights of those other than the buyer and seller in the transaction, or 'incumbrances', as they encumber or burden the land. Third party rights include the following instances.

Easements

An easement is a right to use someone else's land in a particular way. The most common easement is probably a right of way, that is, a right to pass across someone else's land, sometimes on foot and sometimes with vehicles, depending upon the terms. Rights for drains and other services to pass through land are also common, or you may come across a right of light, that is, a right for the light to a window to pass without obstruction over the land of another.

If you buy land subject to an easement, you must not impede the exercise of that right in any way, for example by obstructing a right of way or building so as to diminish a right to light.

When buying land you must find out about any easements affecting it and make sure they will not interfere with your planned use of the land. Equally, you must receive any easements necessary for your enjoyment of the land, for example a right for your drains to pass through neighbouring land.

Easements affecting a piece of land will usually be set out on the Land Register. If they are not, they may still be binding on a buyer even if he or she is not aware of them.

Mortgages

A mortgage is a contract under which a lender is given wide-ranging rights over a piece of land in return for the loan. If you do not comply with the terms of the loan, for example you fail to keep the repayments up to date, a lender (or mortgagee) is allowed to take possession of the property and sell it in order to recover the loan. When buying land, make sure that all mortgages affecting it are paid off in full on completion; otherwise, you will become liable for the repayment of the loan.

To be binding upon a buyer, mortgages must be set out on the Land Register.

Covenants

A covenant is simply a promise made in a deed (a formal legal document). Covenants can either be positive, that is, a promise to carry out work such as repairing a fence; or restrictive, in which the covenant restricts the use of the land in a particular way, for example for residential purposes only.

If you buy a house and a previous owner has entered into a restrictive covenant such as promising not to use the land for commercial purposes, then you will be bound by that covenant even though you have never made any such promise. If you break the covenant you can be sued by the person in whose favour the promise was made – usually a neighbouring landowner.

However, if you buy land subject to a positive covenant, it cannot be directly enforced against you by the person in whose favour the covenant was originally made. That said, it is likely that your seller will require you to promise to comply with the positive covenant and compensate him or her if he or she suffers loss due to your failure to comply (see 'Indemnity Covenants', on page 35).

If the covenant is to pay towards the maintenance of a right of way or other easement that you have the right to use, the law will not allow you to use the easement unless you also accept the obligation to maintain it.

Rights of occupiers

People other than the owner of the land may be in occupation of it or may have rights of occupation over it, and this can cause problems to both buyers and sellers as described below.

In cases where the matrimonial home is owned solely by one spouse, the other spouse is given a right to occupy it under the Family Law Act 1996. This is to prevent the owning spouse selling the house without informing the other. This right is only binding on the buyer if it is entered on the Land Register. However, a non-owning spouse can register his or her right at any time prior to completion of the sale of the house, and it is therefore essential that if you are buying from a single spouse you obtain written confirmation from the non-owning spouse that he or she will not make such a registration and will vacate the house prior to completion.

This right is available only to spouses. It does not include cohabitants of the owner, no matter how long they may have lived in the house. However, under the Land Registration Act 2002, the rights of any person in occupation of the land will usually be binding on a buyer, without the need for them to be entered on the Land Register. If you find out that someone other than or in addition to the seller is in occupation of the house, beware this provision. If someone other than the owner has contributed to the purchase or improvement of a house, for example by helping with the mortgage repayments, then the law may imply that he or she be given a share in the ownership. This rule applies to anyone who makes such contributions, and the right would be binding on a buyer of the land if the person in question was in occupation. The buyer might then have to buy out him or her in order to be able to occupy the house.

So, before buying, you must make very careful enquiries as to who is in occupation of the house. If anyone other than the seller is in occupation, you must get a declaration in writing that he or she will vacate the house prior to completion; the rights cease to be binding if there is no one in occupation on the day of completion (see Chapter 6 for more details on occupiers' rights).

Co-ownership

Closely related to the rules on the rights of occupiers are the rules relating to co-ownership. Co-ownership arises whenever the house is owned (as opposed to just occupied) by more than one person, whether a couple or not. The law draws no distinction here between married couples and unmarried couples. Where there is more than one person registered as proprietor – and this will be clear from the Land Register – then all the owners must join in the sale, and all must sign any documentation.

Problems regarding rights to sell the house can arise where one of the co-owners has died. Two situations can be identified.

1. Where there are still at least two owners alive, they can sell provided they all take part in the sale and that the death certificate of the deceased is produced.

2. Where there is only one co-owner still alive, the situation depends upon the entries on the Land Register. If the Proprietorship Register (see page 38) simply states that A and B were the proprietors, the surviving owner can sell on his or her own on production of the death certificate of the deceased owner. However, if the Proprietorship Register contains either of the following entries:
    *   'RESTRICTION: No disposition by a sole proprietor of the land (not being a trust corporation) under which capital money arises is to be registered except under an order of the Registrar or the Court' or

- 'RESTRICTION: No disposition by a sole proprietor of the registered estate (except a trust corporation) under which capital money arises is to be registered unless authorised under an order of the Court'

then the surviving owner cannot sell on his or her own. There is a danger that the share of the house belonging to the deceased has passed to someone other than the surviving owner and that you as buyer will not be able to obtain full ownership. It will be necessary for the surviving owner to appoint someone to act with him or her in the sale so as to ensure that the land is sold free of anyone else's rights. In such a case you will need to seek legal advice.

However, it will usually be the case that you will find no such restriction on the Register and you can safely buy from the survivor – though you should insist on production of the deceased's death certificate.

Indemnity covenants

When a landowner enters into a covenant, then irrespective of whether future owners of the land will be bound by it, the landowner remains bound by that covenant even after he or she has sold the land (see Example 1, below).

EXAMPLE 1

Charles owns a house and promises his neighbour, Angela (in a deed), that he will not use the house for any purpose other than that of a single private residence. Charles sells the house to Francis. As described earlier on page 33, Francis will be bound by this restrictive covenant. But Charles will also remain bound by it. So if Francis breaks the covenant, for example by converting the house into flats, then Charles can still be sued for breach of the covenant. Angela will have a choice – she can sue either Charles or Francis. If she chooses to sue Charles, Charles could have to pay out damages for breach of this covenant, even though he himself has done nothing wrong.

To protect himself from this injustice, when he sells to Francis, Charles will insist on Francis entering into a covenant in his favour. This will be a covenant to indemnify, that is, compensate Charles in case of any loss caused to him by a future breach of covenant. So if Charles is sued, he can claim from Francis under this indemnity.

When Francis enters into this indemnity covenant, he will remain liable on it, like any other covenant, even after he has sold the house. So if Francis sells to Clare, and Clare breaks the original restrictive covenant and uses the house for commercial purposes, Angela can still sue Charles (even though it may be years since Charles sold the land), and Charles can still sue Francis on the indemnity covenant he entered into with Charles. To protect himself from this, Francis will insist on Clare entering into a similar indemnity arrangement.

So there will develop a chain of indemnity covenants, each seller requiring his or her buyer to enter into such a covenant. As a buyer, therefore, you should expect to enter into such a covenant under such circumstances, and as a seller you should insist on your buyer entering into an indemnity covenant.

Indemnity covenants can be given for both positive and negative covenants. Although the burden of a positive covenant never passes to you as the buyer directly and you can never be sued by the person in whose favour it was made, you may be liable indirectly (see page 35 and Example 2, below). However, the number of occasions where a person has been sued on an indemnity covenant is very few.

EXAMPLE 2

If George enters into a positive covenant with Barry, and George then sells the land to Philippa, Philippa cannot be sued directly by Barry for breach of that covenant. However, George can still be sued and so to protect himself will take an indemnity covenant from Philippa. Thus if Philippa breaks the covenant, Barry can sue George, who can in turn sue Philippa under the indemnity.

Registered land

Most land in England and Wales is registered. This means that details of the ownership of the land are entered on a Register kept by a public agency known as Land Registry. The Registry guarantees that entries are correct, so if the Register states that a particular person is the owner of a piece of land, you can generally rely on that being so (subject to the rights of anyone in occupation – see above). Until 13 October 2003 proprietors of registered land were given a 'Land Certificate' as evidence of their ownership – although if there was a mortgage on the property, the lender would be given a 'Charge Certificate' instead. These are no longer issued for registrations made on or after 13 October 2003, but the proprietor is given a 'Title Information Document' containing copies of the entries on the register.

If the ownership of land is not yet on the Register the rules of law relating to this are more complicated, and sales or purchases of unregistered land should not be undertaken by someone doing their own conveyancing.

Land Registry is organised on a regional basis, with each of 24 district offices containing details of the land in the area assigned to it (see Appendix I). The Registry is open to public inspection (on payment of a fee) and all changes in the ownership of land must be registered to be legally effective. It also contains details of many (but not all) of the third party rights affecting it.

Each title to land is given a separate title number and this must be used to refer to the land in any correspondence with Land Registry. If there is a lease affecting a piece of land, this will be given a separate title number to the freehold.

Form of the register

A specimen of what the Register looks like, in the form of a set of Official Copy Entries, is set out in Appendix II. Official Copy Entries are copies of the Register made by or authorised by Land Registry and it is these that are used to prove ownership of the land. Until October 2003, Official Copy Entries were known as 'office copies' and you may still find them referred to as such. The Register for each title is divided into three parts, each also known as 'registers'. Information about different aspects of the title is kept in each register.

Property Register

The Property Register states whether the land is freehold or leasehold – remember that in the case of leasehold, you will not be able to do your own conveyancing due to the complications of leasehold land. It will also describe the land, both in words by reference to the postal address and by reference to a plan. This is called the 'title plan' and is based on the Ordnance Survey. Until October 2003 it was called the 'filed plan'. In addition, the Property Register will include details of any rights the owner enjoys over other land, for example rights of way and other easements over neighbouring land, and details of any easements to which the property is subject. Remember, however, that if a house is subject to easements, these will be binding upon you as the buyer even if they do not appear on the register.

Proprietorship Register

This Register names the owner(s) or proprietor(s) of the house, and gives a 'class' of title. This will be either 'absolute', 'possessory', 'qualified', or, in the case of leasehold land, 'good leasehold'. Although the Land Registry guarantees that its entries are correct, there are in fact conditions and exceptions. Absolute title gives the fullest guarantee, but you will need to seek expert advice if the title you are buying or selling is registered under any other class of title. The vast majority of freehold land is registered with absolute title.

Restrictions on the proprietor's rights to deal with the land will also be set out in the Proprietorship Register. If you see an entry prefixed 'Caution' or 'Inhibition', seek immediate professional advice as this implies that there may be a serious legal problem to be resolved before the sale can proceed. However, these entries are very rare.

You may also come across entries prefixed 'Restriction'. Such an entry is usually in relation to co-ownership (see page 34), and causes problems only if one of two or more co-owners is still alive. If two of the registered proprietors are alive, the restriction can be ignored. Again, if you encounter any other restriction – for example in relation to bankruptcy, seek professional advice.

Notification of indemnity covenants in the Proprietorship Register is often set out in the following clause:

- 'Note: the Transfer to the proprietors contains a covenant to observe and perform and a covenant for indemnity in respect of the covenants referred to in entry number 1 of the Charges register.'

This tells you that the owner of the land entered into an indemnity covenant when he or she bought the land. A seller will expect you to enter into a similar covenant when you buy the land from him or her. If you are the seller, make sure your buyer enters into such a covenant (see 'Indemnity covenants', on page 35).

Charges Register

This is where most of the third party rights (incumbrances) can be found. It is likely that the first entry will be a mortgage. You will see on the example Official Copy form (Appendix II) that entries numbered 2 and 3 are a mortgage (or 'registered charge') in favour of Humbershire and Counties Bank. Despite the two entry numbers, there is only one mortgage here, but all mortgages must be paid off on or before completion.

Another entry on this Register will relate to restrictive covenants affecting the land (see the example). As a buyer, you should read these carefully as they will be binding on you if you decide to proceed with the purchase. Older covenants may be written in unwieldy legalese – but with a little care and perhaps a dictionary you will be able to decipher what the covenants mean and what restrictions they will place on you if you buy the land. Note, however, that most covenants will simply require you to use the land for residential purposes and not cause a nuisance or annoyance to neighbouring property owners.

In the unlikely event that you come across any entries other than the types described here, you will need to seek professional advice.

Overriding interests

The Land Register should set out all the burdens in favour of other people which affect the land. However, some rights are considered so important that they are binding even though they are not on the register. These overriding interests bind the owner, and his or her buyer, even if they have no knowledge of the existence of the rights.

Although this may sound a little worrying, in reality overriding interests do not normally cause any problems in residential conveyancing, provided you follow the basic precautions, outlined in Chapters 4 and 6. Doing your own conveyancing will not put you at a disadvantage when dealing with overriding interests, as a conveyancer is in no better position than you to find out what they are; a careful inspection of the property should reveal any over-riding interests, but this will not normally be carried out by a conveyancer as part of the conveyancing process.

Overriding interests for which you should take special precautions in a house purchase are as follows:

- **the rights of any person in occupation of the land** (see page 33) You will thus need to make sure that there is no one else in occupation of the house other than the seller. If there is, you will need to ensure that they agree to vacate on completion.
- **easements such as rights of way and drainage** Again, as a buyer you will need to inspect the land to see if there are any easements affecting it.

The District Land Registry Office

There are 24 Land Registry Offices throughout England and Wales, each responsible for a designated area of the country. Always send all correspondence, forms and so on relating to a house to the correct office, that is, the one which deals with the land in that area. Details of which Land Registry deals with which area and addresses for all the Land Registry Offices can be found in Appendix I. These change from time to time, but up-to-date information can be obtained from any Office, or Land Registry's website at *www.landreg.gov.uk*.

Land Registry's website also contains other useful information about the land registration system, including the forms necessary to obtain information or make entries on the register. They can be downloaded free. The information is presented in a user-friendly format and an hour spent browsing the site will be very useful and informative to any house owner.

Although it is possible to view the Register on-line (on payment of a fee, currently £2, by credit card), at *www.landregisteronline.gov.uk/*, it is not possible to obtain official copies or make any applications this way. However, conveyancers and other professionals can make use of Land Registry Direct, which enables applications and so on to be dealt with by direct computer links.

If you do not have access to the Internet, each Land Registry Office has an Enquiry Desk to deal with queries, either in person or over the phone, but you cannot expect the staff there to deal with any specific legal problems.

Wales

Conveyancing documents for properties in Wales can be completed in either English or Welsh. Land Registry forms are also available in either English or Welsh. Land Registry will make the entries on the Register in the same language as the documents by which the transaction was carried out. If you are a Welsh speaker and the entries on the Register are in English, Land Registry will provide a Welsh translation on request. Similarly, if the Register entries are in Welsh, Land Registry will provide an English translation if required. Note, however, that it is not possible for Welsh expatriates living in England to deal with properties in England in the Welsh language.

Basic contract law

To be legally enforceable, a contract relating to the sale of land must satisfy the following conditions:

- it must be in writing
- it must contain all the terms agreed to by both parties
- it must be signed by both parties
- both parties must intend it to be a legally binding agreement.

Therefore, the verbal agreement when a buyer finds a house he or she wants to buy and the seller accepts the offer is not legally binding; either party can still walk away without recrimination.

It is essential that the written contract prepared and signed by the parties includes all that has been agreed verbally, otherwise it will not be a legally binding contract. Although there will be much written correspondence between buyer and seller prior to exchange, the law generally assumes that neither party wishes this to be binding until contracts are exchanged in the usual way, thus eliminating the risk of any such correspondence being construed as a binding contract. A further safety measure is the addition of the disclaimer heading 'subject to contract' on preliminary correspondence, which states that the letter cannot be used to bind the sender to a contract prior to exchange.

As mentioned earlier in this chapter (see page 29), a contract for the sale of land is usually entered into by exchange of contracts. In this case the law is as follows:

- the contract is entered into only on exchange of the two parts, not on signature
- both copies of the contract must be identical; if they are not there can be no binding contract even if exchange takes place
- the buyer signs one copy and the seller the other; there is no need for both parties to sign both copies.

Where contracts are exchanged at a personal meeting, the contract becomes binding as soon as the last part is handed over. If contracts are exchanged through the post, the Form of Contract incorporating the Standard Conditions of Sale (see page 53) make it clear that the contract becomes binding when the last part is posted, not on its receipt by the other party.

Stamp duty land tax

This replaced stamp duty as from 1 December 2003. Details of most property transactions now have to be reported to the Inland Revenue on a new type of tax return. It is the responsibility of the buyer to make the tax return and pay the tax. Tax is only payable on the purchase price of the house and not on any carpets, curtains and so on included in the sale. It can, therefore, be beneficial expressly to allocate part of the price as payment for chattels in order to save duty (see page 67). Tax is chargeable as follows.

Where the total price paid (in money or otherwise) is:

- up to £60,000   – the rate of duty is 0%
- over £60,000 up to £250,000   – the rate of duty is 1% of the total price paid
- over £250,000 up to £500,000   – the rate of duty is 3% of the total price paid
- over £500,000   – the rate of duty is 4% of the total price paid.

However, if the house is in a 'disadvantaged area', as defined by the government, then no duty becomes payable until the price paid exceeds £150,000.

See page 139 for details of the Land Transaction Return and how to pay the duty.

Warning

There is an old saying that 'a little knowledge is a dangerous thing', and this is particularly true of the law. Do not assume that because you have read this chapter you are now an expert on the law relating to the sale and purchase of houses – you are not! The chapter only sets out the barest bones of the law; if you come across anything you do not understand or are unsure of, you should obtain professional advice.

Chapter 4

Selling your house – finding a buyer to exchange of contracts

Having decided to do your own conveyancing, the next vital step is to plan ahead. Read through all the chapters of this book dealing with the sale of a house before you put the house on the market, and be sure that you understand what is involved in doing the work yourself. You will not have time once you have started the process to work out what happens at each stage; any delay might cost you the sale or result in you being in breach of contract and having to pay compensation to the buyer.

To start, you should buy all the forms you are likely to need during the transaction *before* putting the house on the market (see page 47). Again, you may not have time to find and buy a particular form halfway through the transaction.

The longest part of a conveyancing transaction is the time between finding a buyer and the buyer actually entering into a legally binding contract. This can easily take six weeks or more, and it is the length of this delay that enables gazumping or gazundering (according to the state of the property market) to flourish.

This delay also gives a buyer time in which to change his or her mind and decide to buy something else. Remember, as a legally binding contract does not exist until exchange, if either party decides not to proceed, there is no comeback and no compensation for the expense and inconvenience to the other party.

It is therefore to everybody's advantage if contracts can be exchanged as soon as possible. As seller, you can speed things up by having your pre-contract package prepared and ready to send out as soon as the buyer is found and the sale agreed. Indeed, you may wish to pre-empt the government's legislation on Home Information Packs and prepare your own voluntarily. You could include in this all the searches that a buyer would normally make prior to exchange of contracts (see page 105). Presenting these to the buyer right at the start of the transaction might reduce the delay prior to exchange and thus speed things up.

Financial matters

Before putting your house on the market, you will need to ensure that the amount you get for the sale of the house is enough to cover:

- all your existing mortgages
- the lender's conveyancer's fees (plus VAT)
- your estate agent's fees (plus VAT)
- the cost of your forms (see page 47)
- removal costs (plus VAT).

Also, if you are buying another house, that you have sufficient funds to do this. If you are involved in a sale *and* purchase you should also consider carefully the guidance given in Chapter 6.

Existing mortgages

If you are selling but not buying at the same time, bear in mind that any and all mortgages secured against the house will have to be paid off in full out of the proceeds of the sale. Therefore, there must be sufficient funds available from the sale, after payment of all expenses, to cover this. If you are selling up to live in a mobile home or to live abroad, for example, sufficient funds must be left for you to be able to afford to do so.

Take into your calculations the following:

- **the price you can realistically expect for the house** This is not the original asking price, but the amount the estate agent advises you may have to settle for. In many parts of the country, this may not be a problem as house prices are, at the time of writing, increasing rapidly. However, in other parts of the country the housing market is still very sluggish. Rely on your estate agent for guidance.

- **the estate agent's fees** Do not forget to add on VAT at 17.5 per cent and any extra costs for advertising, providing a sale board and so on.

- **amount outstanding on the mortgage(s)** Look at the latest annual mortgage statement provided by your lender(s), as this will give you a rough idea of what is outstanding. If you do not have a recent one, contact the lender. At the time of writing, negative equity (where the house is worth less than the amount of the loan) is probably a thing of the past in most parts of England and Wales owing to recent rises in house prices, but check carefully that the sale proceeds will cover all loans secured against the house. If you enter into a contract to sell you will be promising to pay off all mortgages on that house, and if you then discover that you are unable to do so, you will be in breach of contract and liable to pay substantial damages. Check especially carefully where you have more than one mortgage secured on the house – and particularly where one of the loans was only recently taken out.

  Do not forget the terms of the original loan. If you took advantage of a special offer when taking out the loan, for example a fixed-rate or cashback loan, it may be that one of the terms specifies that if you wish to pay off the loan within a certain period of borrowing the money, you must pay an extra repayment charge over and above the amount outstanding. This may be a fixed sum, such as the repayment of the cashback you received on taking out the loan, or a percentage of the amount borrowed, such as 2 per cent. Check this carefully with your lender before putting the house on the market in order to avoid any unpleasant surprises.

- **other fees payable to the lender** Most lenders will charge a deeds fee, that is, a fee for sending the deeds to a conveyancer so that they can be handed over to the buyer on completion. They will also charge a sealing fee for 'sealing' or signing the document required to be handed over to the buyer to certify that the loan has been paid off. These fees vary between lenders, but you should allow around £100 to cover both.

- **lender's conveyancer's fees** The deeds which need to be handed over to the buyer on completion (see above) will be in the possession of the lender, and, even if you are doing your own conveyancing, the lender will not release the deeds to you until the loan has been repaid. Equally, the buyer will not hand over the purchase price (which you will be using to repay the loan) unless he or she receives the deeds in return. This 'Catch 22' situation is resolved by the lender sending the deeds to a conveyancer who promises to hold on to them until he or she has received the amount outstanding on the loan. The downside of this is that you will have to pay the lender's conveyancer's fees, which are likely to be in the region of between £120 to £200, plus VAT.

Buying the forms

You will need to obtain the following forms:

- Land Registry Form SIM (but see 'Index Map Search', below) (one copy)
- Land Registry Form OC1 (one copy)
- Form of Contract incorporating the Standard Conditions of Sale[†] (two copies)
- Seller's Property Information Form[†] (two copies)
- Fixtures, Fittings and Contents Form (two copies)
- If you are planning to prepare a Home Information Pack to send to the buyer, you will also need copies of the various search forms that a buyer would normally use (see page 89).
- ([†] Alternatively, you can prepare your own versions of these – see page 156.)

Although only one or two copies of the forms are required, it may be useful to obtain some spares just in case you have a problem completing them. You may also find that you are unable to buy a single copy of a form, as they are often sold in packs of five.

Where to buy the forms

Legal forms will be available from a law stationers – look in the *Yellow Pages* for a local firm. Alternatively, Oyez Straker★ offers an on-line and a telephone ordering service. However, Land Registry Forms SIM and OC1 (see example forms in Appendix II) can be downloaded free of charge from Land Registry's website at *www.landreg.gov.uk*.

Preparing the pre-contract package

Remember, the pre-contract package should be prepared *before* you have found a buyer.

Is the house registered at Land Registry?

The first thing you will need to do is to make sure your house is registered at Land Registry. If the land is unregistered, then you will need to instruct a conveyancer.

Houses are being added to the Register gradually. If you acquired the house recently, or it is in an urban area, it is likely to be registered. If you acquired the house more than 20 years ago, and it is in a rural area, then it may not yet be registered.

You may well remember whether your house was registered or not when you bought it. Alternatively, if the house is not subject to a mortgage, you will have the deeds in your possession – or preferably in safe-keeping somewhere. If the deeds contain a 'Land Certificate' or a 'Title Information Document', the land is registered.

Index Map Search

If you cannot remember whether your house is registered or not, then you can do an Index Map Search at Land Registry. The map is based on the Ordnance Survey covering all the land in England and Wales, and shows whether or not the land is registered. If you know that the house is registered, but do not know the title number, there is no need to do this search (see 'Official Copy Entries', below).

The search is completed on Form SIM (see Appendix II).

The form is quite straightforward and contains seven boxes to complete. You will also need to complete the box at the top of the page with the name and address of the appropriate Land Registry Office. For the relevant Land Registry Office to which this form should be sent and the addresses, see Appendix I.

A fee of £4 was previously payable for this search, but at the time of writing Land Registry is waiving payment of this fee, so you can ignore the 'Payment of Fee' box on the form.

You need to include details of the land to be searched against in Box 6. If the property can be readily identified from its postal address – as most established houses can be – then a plan is not necessary.

On the return of the search, Land Registry will advise whether or not the land is registered and if so the title number. If the result discloses any information other than that the land is registered freehold (and the title number), **you will not be able to do your own conveyancing as you will need professional advice on the implications of the entries.**

Official Copy Entries

Having ascertained that the land is registered, you now need up-to-date copies of the entries on the Land Register, in order to draft the sale contract and to send to the buyer to prove to him or her that you do indeed own the land. Even if you have the Land Certificate in your possession (which contains copies of the entries), you will still need to obtain the Official Copy Entries as you are obliged to send these to the buyer.

Official Copy Entries can be obtained by completing Land Registry Form OC1 and sending it together with the appropriate fee to the appropriate Land Registry Office. You do not need the title number to obtain these Official Copy Entries.

If you have the Land Certificate, the title number will be clearly stated on the copy entries inside the certificate; the title number will also be included in the results of an Index Map Search (see above) if it revealed that the land is registered. If you know the land is registered but do not know the title number, Land Registry will look it up for you and at the moment no extra fee is paid for this.

Form OC1 is shown in Appendix II.

Checking the Official Copy Entries

On receipt of the Official Copy Entries (they should not take more than a few days to be returned), you will need to check them carefully. Example Official Copy Entries are found in Appendix II. Check that your Official Copy Entries comply with the following conditions, otherwise you will not be able to do your own conveyancing:

- **that the description of the land in the Property Register is correct** This should be the current postal address of the house with reference to the plan filed at Land Registry; it may also include details of rights benefiting the house and obligations to which it is subject, for example rights of way or drainage. This is quite normal

- **that you are registered as the proprietor of the land**
- **that the class of title is absolute** (see page 38) If it is registered under any other class of title, you will not be able to do your own conveyancing
- **that there are no 'cautions' or 'restrictions' registered on the Proprietorship Register** (These will be entries prefixed

---

Completing Form OC1

You will need to insert the name and address of the appropriate Land Registry Office in the top left. To find out which Land Registry Office the form should be sent to and the address, see Appendix I.
The rest of the boxes on Form OC1 are numbered:

Box 1 – insert the name of the county or unitary council within which the house is situated.

Box 2 – insert the title number, if known; if not, leave blank and type at the top of the form 'Please supply title number'.

Box 3 – insert the address of the property.

Box 4 – place an X in the first box; the fee of £8 accompanies the form.

Box 5 – insert your name and address. Ignore the reference to the Land Registry key number; this is for credit account holders.

Box 6 – leave this blank; you will want the copies to be sent to your own address.

Box 7 – place an X in the first box. Your application relates to the freehold.

Box 8 – place an X in the second box.

Box 9 – place an X in the first two boxes – i.e., you require official copies of the Register AND the title plan.

You will then need to sign and date the form.

by the word 'Caution' or 'Restriction'.) However, if one of the two following restrictions is registered, then you can still do your own conveyancing provided that none of the owners of the land has died:

- 'RESTRICTION: No disposition by a sole proprietor of the land (not being a trust corporation) under which capital money arises is to be registered except under an order of the Registrar or the Court' or

- 'RESTRICTION: No disposition by a sole proprietor of the registered estate (except a trust corporation) under which capital money arises is to be registered unless authorised under an order of the Court.'

This simply means that on the death of one of the owners, the surviving owner cannot sell on his or her own. Provided that all the registered owners are alive and agree to the sale, there is no problem. However, if one of the owners has died, then professional advice will be required

- **that you have not broken any of the covenants set out in the Charges Register** Many houses will have covenants restricting the use of the property, or restricting or prohibiting alterations or extensions to the property. Make sure that you have not broken any of the obligations set out in the charges register. If you have, it is likely that the buyer will require you to remedy the breach before being willing to proceed with the purchase. So if there is a covenant not to build an extension without a named person's consent, and you have done so, then consent must be obtained retrospectively. Covenants usually require the consent of the named owner of an adjoining piece of land. If that named owner has died or has simply sold the land, consent will then be needed from the present owner(s) of the stated piece of land.

  If you have broken one of the covenants within the last six years, take professional advice as to what remedial steps will be required to make the property saleable.

  If you broke a covenant more than six years ago, it is unlikely that this will cause a problem with the sale, but you will need to insert a special provision in the contract (see page 55). The buyer may also require you to take out insurance in respect of the breach (see page 68).

Missing covenants

It is usually the case that the covenants affecting the land will be set out in full in the Charges Register. When you send the Official Copy Entries to the buyer he or she will be able to see what the covenants are and decide how to proceed with the purchase. It is rare that covenants cause a problem when selling a house as they usually simply restrict the use of the property, for example for residential use only. Some of them may be written in archaic legal language, but you should be able to decipher these with the aid of a good dictionary.

However, the details of the covenants are sometimes missing. If this is the case, the Register will state that the land is subject to covenants created in a particular deed, but that no copy of them was produced on first registration. Technically, as you are aware of the existence of the covenants, you are bound by them – even though you do not know what exactly they are. Missing covenants might therefore be of concern to a buyer; if it is not known what the covenants are, it is very difficult to be certain that they have not been, or will not be, broken. However, provided they were created in the dim and distant past – say, more than 50 years ago – they should not create a problem on the sale. It is likely, however, that the buyer will require you to take out insurance (see page 68). So, for example, if you have carried out building work on the land or changed its use, there may be a chance that you have inadvertently broken the covenants. Most missing covenants date back 60 years or more, and the chances of anyone suing on them now are remote.

Existing mortgages

If you have an existing mortgage on the house, this will be entered as a Registered Charge in the Charges Register. You will need to pay off all mortgages out of the proceeds of the sale, ensuring that there will be sufficient funds to do this (see page 45). You will need to advise the lender that you are selling the house and will therefore be paying off the loan.

The lender will require a conveyancer to act on its behalf in connection with the repayment of the loan. The lender will then send any documents it is holding to the conveyancer, who will hand them over to the buyer on completion. Most lenders will allow you to nominate this conveyancer and you will be expected to pay the fees.

Ring around for a quote, explaining that you are selling and handling the legal work on the sale yourself and that the quote is for redemption of the mortgage only. If you ask the lender to nominate the conveyancer you will have no advance estimate of the fee payable.

If there is more than one mortgage on the house, all of them will have to be paid off and it is wise to make sure that the same conveyancer acts for both lenders in connection with paying off the loans. However, some finance companies will insist on their own conveyancer and this could again increase the cost.

Drafting the contract using the Form of Contract incorporating the Standard Conditions of Sale

Your most important job when doing your own conveyancing is to draft the contract for the sale. You will need two copies of the Form of Contract incorporating the Standard Conditions of Sale. If you have been unable to obtain this form, see 'Drafting the contract – your own Form of Agreement' on page 56. The form should be completed as follows.

Date – leave blank, this will be inserted on exchange.

Seller – your name and address; if there is more than one owner, for example your spouse or partner, then all the names should be inserted.

Buyer – if a buyer has not yet been found, leave this blank and complete with the buyer's name and address when it is known.

Property – delete 'Leasehold'; remember, if your house is leasehold, you will not be able to do your own conveyancing. Insert the details of the house you are selling. This should be copied word for word from the Property Register as set out in the Official Copy Entries. If the Property Register includes lengthy details of rights benefiting or affecting the property, usually prefixed by words such as 'Together with but subject to ...', do not include these here.

Root of Title/Title Number – delete 'Root of Title'. Insert the title number from the Official Copy Entries and follow that with 'registered with Absolute Title'.

Specified Incumbrances – insert 'The Property is sold subject to the entries on the Register (except entry numbers [ ] and [ ] in the Charges Register)'. If there is no Registered Charge (that is, a mortgage) on the property, the part in brackets can be omitted; if there are any Registered Charges, the buyer will not wish to buy subject to these and they will need paying off on completion (see page 52). You will see from the example Official Copy Entries in Appendix II that each mortgage has two entry numbers, one indicating there is a registered charge, the other stating the name of the lender. Both entry numbers for all mortgages on the property should be inserted to make it clear that the buyer is not buying subject to these and that you will pay them off on completion.

Title Guarantee – delete 'Limited'.

Completion Date – leave blank; this will be agreed and inserted on exchange.

Contract Rate – leave blank; the Standard Conditions will then imply the Law Society's interest rate, which is 4 per cent above the Barclays Bank base rate. This interest rate becomes of relevance if there is a delay in completion, when compensation is payable to the non-delaying party and is calculated as interest on the purchase price for the period of delay (see Chapter 9).

Purchase Price – you will need to leave this blank until a sale has been agreed, when you should insert the agreed price.

Deposit – this should be 10 per cent of the purchase price AND any separate price agreed for chattels – see 'Chattels Price', next.

Chattels Price – when a sale is agreed, insert any separate sum agreed for carpets, curtains and so on. Whether or not a separate sum has been initially agreed, the buyer may wish to allocate a price for chattels in order to save stamp duty land tax (see page 67).

Balance – again, this can be calculated once a sale has been agreed; it is the purchase price and the chattels price less the deposit, which gives the amount payable on completion.

On the back page of the contract:

Delete Special Condition 3 – ('The chattels which are on the Property…').

Once this condition has been deleted, renumber the remaining Special Condition, so original Condition 4 will become Condition 3.

Original Special Condition 4 (now renumbered Condition 3) has two versions; delete the second alternative, making it clear that the property is sold with vacant possession on completion.

Insert new Special Condition 4 – 'The chattels set out on any attached list are included in the sale; the fixtures on the Property and set out in the same list are excluded from the sale'. See 'Fixtures and Contents Form' on page 56 as to this provision.

Insert new Special Condition 5 – 'Standard Conditions 5.1.1 and 5.1.2 shall not apply to this sale'.

Under these Standard Conditions, the seller bears any loss if the house should be damaged or destroyed between exchange and completion (for example by fire); excluding the conditions places the responsibility on the buyer, who must insure the property to protect against any such loss. Despite this provision, however, you must not cancel your own insurance on the property until completion; you do not want to run the risk of being left with a damaged house if the buyer forgets to insure.

Insert new Special Condition 6 – 'In Standard Condition 2.2.4 reference to the Seller's conveyancer shall be deemed to be a reference to the Seller'.

Condition 2.2.4 refers to the deposit being held by the seller's conveyancer, and so is not appropriate where you are acting on your own behalf. It may well be that the buyer's conveyancer will not be agreeable to you holding the deposit yourself anyway (see page 66 as to the implications of this).

Missing covenants

As explained earlier (see page 52), details of the covenants on the Register are sometimes missing, although this does not normally impede the sale. However, if you are faced with missing covenants, it is essential that you clearly explain this to the buyer. You should therefore insert a special condition stating the following:

'The Seller has no copy of or further information about the covenants referred to in entry No.... of the Charges Register and will accept no requisition or objection in relation to them.'

(You should insert the number of the relevant entry as set out in the Official Copy Entries.) The buyer must then decide whether or not to buy in full possession of the fact that these covenants are missing. Though it is unusual for this to cause problems, the buyer's conveyancer may insist on insurance being obtained (see page 68).

Draft in duplicate

Prepare two identical copies of the agreement; both will need to be sent to the buyer, so also make a photocopy of the agreement to keep in your own file.

Drafting the contract – your own Form of Agreement

If you have been unable to obtain the Form of Contract incorporating the Standard Conditions of Sale, you will need to type/wordprocess your own Form of Contract. This will take you a little longer, but remember, you are doing all this work well in advance of selling the house.

The contract should be set out as shown in the box opposite. However, it is essential that you refer to the above guidance notes on completing the Form of Contract incorporating the Standard Conditions of Sale when drafting your own contract and you should complete your own form in the same way. The Standard Conditions themselves are set out in Appendix II. You need not include the full text of the conditions in your contract form; it is sufficient to refer to them in the contract.

The Standard Conditions contract form includes spaces in which to insert the title guarantee and the contract rate (see page 54). These are not included in this form, but will be implied as being Full Title guarantee and the Law Society's interest rate.

Fixtures and Contents Form

The new Special Condition 4 (Special Condition 2 if you prepare your own form) in the contract refers to fixtures and chattels. Under the law, when you sell a house you do not sell the furniture and other moveable contents (chattels); however, the sale does include fixtures, that is, anything securely fixed to the house.

It is often a difficult legal problem to decide whether various items are fixtures (and so should be left behind when you move) or chattels, which you can take with you. Curtain rails, television aerials, light fittings, for example, are particularly problematical. To save any argument, therefore, it is usual to state clearly precisely what is and is not included in the sale.

You may have bought the printed Fixtures, Fittings and Contents Form, in which case you should complete it (in duplicate) following the guidance set out on the form.

CONTRACT FOR SALE

SELLER

BUYER

PROPERTY

TITLE NUMBER

INCUMBRANCES

COMPLETION DATE

PRICE

DEPOSIT

AMOUNT PAYABLE FOR CHATTELS

BALANCE DUE ON COMPLETION

The Seller agrees to sell and the Buyer agrees to buy the Property at the Price and on the terms set out in this contract.

CONDITIONS OF SALE

This contract incorporates the Standard Conditions of Sale (Fourth Edition) insofar as those Conditions are not altered or varied by or are inconsistent with this Contract.

SPECIAL CONDITION 1 – The Property is sold with vacant possession on completion.

SPECIAL CONDITION 2 – The chattels set out on any attached list are included in the sale; the fixtures on the Property and set out in the same list are excluded from the sale.

SPECIAL CONDITION 3 – Standard Conditions 5.1.1 and 5.1.2 shall not apply to this sale.

SPECIAL CONDITION 4 – In Standard Condition 2.2.4 reference to the Seller's conveyancer shall be deemed to be a reference to the Seller.

(Signed)...

Seller/Buyer

Alternatively, you should type up a form setting out precisely what is and is not included in the sale. This should be headed 'Fixtures and Contents' – an example form and details of how to complete it are set out below. Prepare two identical copies of this form. As both will have to be sent to the buyer, you should also keep a further copy for your own use.

Preliminary Enquiries/Property Information Form

Strictly, a seller of land is under no obligation to provide any information about it other than proof of his or her ownership, that is, the Official Copy Entries. However, it is sensible to provide as

---

Fixtures and Contents Form

This form sets out the items included and excluded from the sale of ... (*insert address of property*) and is incorporated into the contract for the sale of that property.

Included in sale: (*The following are just examples of what might be included/excluded from the sale*)

General

TV aerial	Garden shed
Radio aerial	LPG gas in tank
Doorbell	Outside lights
Burglar alarm	Oil/gas in tank

(*Set out all similar items as appropriate*)

Excluded from sale:
General

Greenhouse	Rotary clothes line
Dustbin	Telephone handset
3 ornamental shrubs	Satellite dish
Garden seat	

(*Set out all similar items as appropriate*)

Sitting room
Then list ALL the other rooms in your house, e.g.:

Bedroom 1	Bedroom 2 etc.

---

much information as possible in order to speed up the transaction. You should therefore complete a Preliminary Enquiries/Enquiries before Contract/Property Information Form. These are all different names for the same thing – a list of questions about the property.

Although you do not have to answer these questions, it is usual to do so and it would certainly be viewed with suspicion if you refused. It is wise to provide answers to the usual questions as part of your pre-contract package to avoid any delay.

You may be able to buy the printed Seller's Property Information Form from a law stationer. Two copies will be required – one for yourself and one for the buyer. You should then complete this

---

For each room decide which of the following is included/excluded from the sale and insert in the appropriate list:

curtain rails	venetian (or other) blinds
curtains	gas/electric fire
pelmets	storage radiators
light fittings (if light fittings are	carpets (or other floor covering)
excluded, indicate whether you	fitted cupboards/wardrobes/
will be leaving the ceiling rose	bedroom units
and lamp holder)	shelving
light bulbs	

For the kitchen/utility room you should also consider:

fitted cupboards	microwave oven
refrigerator	tumble drier
freezer	towel rail
dishwasher	shelves
washing machine	wall-mounted can opener
oven/cooker/hob	any other items fixed to the
extractor fan/cooker hood	walls or cupboards

In addition, for the bathroom (and any other lavatory):

shelves	bathroom cabinet
towel rails	mirror
toilet roll holder	lavatory seat
soap/toothbrush holder	

following the guidance on the form. It is designed to be completed by the seller, rather than by the seller's conveyancer. There are also various other similar Preliminary Enquiries forms published. As there are various types of the form available, it is not possible here to give guidance on completion.

Alternatively, you could prepare your own form (see pages 62–3). Whatever option you choose, you must be completely truthful in what you say, avoiding half-truths or clever forms of words which suggest one thing but mean another. The buyer will partly base his or her decision on whether to buy on your answers, and if these prove to be untrue or misleading then he or she will have the right to withdraw from the purchase and claim compensation from you. If you do not know the answer to a question you should say so – do not guess. The form should be signed at the end by yourself and any other owner of the house, that is, any co-owner as set out in the Proprietorship Register.

Guidance notes

In completing the form, type out the questions as set out and then underneath or in a separate column set out your answers. Your answers should be truthful; if you do not know the answer to a question, or are not sure, you must say so. Common answers might include: 'I am not aware of any'; 'Not to the best of my knowledge'; 'I have no information about this'.

Occupiers

The 'Occupiers' question on the Preliminary Enquiries Form asks whether anyone else apart from yourself or a co-owner lives in the house. If there is such a person you must ensure that he or she is agreeable to the sale taking place and will move out prior to completion. This is not usually a problem as the other occupiers will often be members of your family and moving with you. However, before putting the house on the market make sure that they are agreeable to signing a form stating that they will leave, as follows:

I, [*insert name of occupier*], agree to the sale of [*insert address of house*] with vacant possession. I agree to vacate the house on or before completion of the sale and not to register or assert any rights I may have over the house against the buyer and not in any way to impede or obstruct the sale.

....[signature and date]

Such a form will probably be insisted upon by the buyer (see page 69). But you as seller are also concerned that the occupiers will leave; you are promising the buyer that you are selling with vacant possession and if any occupier refused to leave, you would be in breach of contract and liable to damages.

Note that this form should be signed by all occupiers (including spouses) except children under 16 years old. You must not in any way attempt to 'persuade' an occupier to sign, as this would make the signature not binding upon him or her. If anyone has any doubts about signing you should recommend that they obtain legal advice as to their rights.

Other documents

You will see that the Preliminary Enquiries Form asks whether you have any guarantees in relation to the house or any work carried out, for example cavity wall insulation. If you have any such documents, make a copy ready to send to the buyer with the rest of the pre-contract package. If you cannot find any guarantees in relation to work done, say so on the form; this should not cause a problem.

However, an essential guarantee is the National House Building Council (NHBC)★ Buildmark guarantee given by the builder on a new house. (There are other similar guarantees, such as Foundation 15, which are equally acceptable.) If you are selling a house built within the last ten years, the buyer (and his or her lender) will insist on the house being protected by the NHBC or a similar structural guarantee. This guarantee is usually kept with the title deeds. If there is no mortgage on the house, you will have the deeds in your possession and will be able to check whether there is such a certificate. A copy of this should be sent to the buyer as part of the pre-contract package.

However, if there is a mortgage on the property, the deeds will be kept by the lender. As explained earlier (see page 46), the lender will not let you have them until the loan has been paid off, and will send them to a conveyancer who will act on behalf of the lender in connection with repaying the loan. You should, therefore, contact

Preliminary Enquiries Form

1. Disputes with Neighbours

Do you know of any disputes with the owners or occupiers of any neighbouring property?

If so, give details.

2. Fences and other Boundary Markers

State who is responsible for maintaining each wall, fence or other boundary marker at the property.

If you do not know who is responsible, which ones have you actually maintained?

Has any boundary marker been moved during the last 12 years?

3. Services

Which of the following mains services are connected to the property?

Gas, electricity, water, drains, telephone, cable television.

Do the pipes, wires etc. for these cross anyone else's property?

Do any pipes, wires etc. leading to another property cross your property?

Do you know of any arrangement regarding these services?

If there is no mains drainage, what arrangements are there for drainage (e.g. septic tank)?

Is gas or oil delivered to a tank on the property?

If so, who owns the tank?

4. Shared Facilities

Do you have to contribute towards the cost of any facilities (e.g. pipes, drains, rights of access) used jointly with others?

If so, give details of payments made, i.e. amounts and to whom.

Do you need to go on to other property in order to maintain part of your property?

If so, have you had any problems in so doing?

Do any neighbours need to come on to the property to maintain their property?

If so, has the exercise of this right ever caused any disputes?

5. Building Work

Have you carried out any building work on the property during the past four years?

If yes, was planning consent, Building Regulation approval and Listed Building consent obtained? Please supply copies, if relevant. Were any other consents required for the building work, e.g. under a restriction set out on the Register?

If so, please supply a copy of the consent.

Have there been any changes in the use of the property over the past ten years? (Including conversion into more than one dwelling.) If yes, was planning permission obtained? Please supply copies, if relevant.

6. Guarantees

Is the property covered by any of the following types of guarantee?

- Damp-proof course
- Double glazing
- Central heating
- Cavity wall insulation
- Wood worm/dry rot or similar
- Roofing or other building work
- Structural Guarantee given by original builder, e.g. NHBC

Please supply copies.

7. Notices

Have you received any notices or letters in relation to the property or your use of it?

Please supply copies.

8. Occupiers

Does anyone else other than yourself live in the property?

If yes, give their full names and ages.

this conveyancer and ask for written confirmation that there is an NHBC certificate with the deeds. You can then send a copy of the written confirmation to the buyer's conveyancer as part of the pre-contract package.

If your house was individually designed and built, this may have been under the supervision of an architect. If there is no NHBC cover, there may be a certificate from the architect providing an independent guarantee against structural defects, and this will normally be acceptable to a buyer. It is usually kept with the deeds and a copy should be prepared to send to the buyer.

Planning permission and Building Regulations

The various preliminary enquiry forms also ask about building work carried out within the last four years. Planning permission from the district council is required for most building work and the buyer will insist on seeing this. The four-year time limit is laid down, as outside that period it is then too late for the local authority to bring proceedings for failure to obtain permission. Note, however, that if a change of use took place, then the local authority can bring proceedings within ten years of the change of use. Also, to ensure that building work is carried out safely, Building Regulation consent is required from the building inspector of the district council. Because of recent court cases, it is likely that a buyer will insist on seeing Building Regulation consent in respect of all building work carried out since the house was built. If there is no such consent with the deeds, then the local authority may be able to help. However, many local councils do not keep records going back more than a few years. If the council cannot help, then it is likely that the buyer will insist on your taking out insurance to cover against any possible breach of the Regulations.

When a buyer is found

As soon as a buyer has been found, you will need to insert the details of the buyer and the sale price in the draft contract (see page 53). Then check the other documents you have prepared and ensure that the contents are still correct. This is particularly important if they were prepared some time ago; remember that any errors in the documentation could at the very least lead to a delay in the sale, and at worst to the sale falling through and substantial damages becoming payable.

The pre-contract package should be sent to the buyer (or his or her conveyancer if you know who this is), with a covering letter (see box on page 73 for a suggested letter). The package should include:

- two copies of the draft contract
- two copies of the Fixtures and Contents Form
- one copy of the Preliminary Enquiries Form
- the Official Copy Entries and title plan
- copies of any structural guarantees, planning permissions and so on referred to in the Preliminary Enquiries Form.

Make sure that you keep copies of all the above documents for your own use.

Waiting for the buyer

Once you have sent the pre-contract package to the buyer, he or she will need to make various searches and enquiries about the property, and make sure that his or her finances are in order, and so there will be some delay before contracts can be exchanged.

Buyer's queries

The buyer may ask for more information from you. Even though you have supplied answers to the Preliminary Enquiries Form, many firms of conveyancers have their own form of enquiries that they raise and will send this to you. Answer the questions honestly to the best of your knowledge. You are obliged to answer only those questions regarding your ownership of the land, but co-operation with the buyer in answering any other questions will speed up the transaction. However, do not answer any questions about the structural state of the house. If the buyer asks for confirmation that there are no structural defects (either in general terms or in relation to a specific matter), simply reply that the buyer should rely on his or her own survey. The buyer will rely on any statement you make and it is dangerous for someone not qualified as a surveyor to make pronouncements on the structural state of the property.

Approval of the draft contract

The buyer needs to approve the terms of the contract as drafted by you, and may wish to negotiate some of the terms, for example what is or is not included in the sale. Although this type of query is fairly straightforward, the following need special consideration.

The deposit

Although it is usual to request a 10 per cent deposit, the buyer may not be in a position to fund such a large amount. The buyer will often be relying on the deposit paid over to him or her on the sale of his or her existing house, and this is likely to be less than you require. It is perfectly in order to agree to a request that the deposit be reduced provided that a substantial sum is still being paid over (for example, 5 per cent of the purchase price). However, if you are also intending to use this deposit as the deposit on a house you are buying, you will need to consider the effect that such a reduced deposit will have on that purchase. There is no point in agreeing to the payment of a reduced deposit only to find that you cannot now fund the deposit on your own purchase, and so you will need to liaise with the sellers of the house you are buying to ensure that they will also accept a reduced deposit.

A buyer may also be reluctant to allow you to hold the deposit yourself. Should you become bankrupt between exchange and completion and the sale fall through, there is a danger that the buyer will be unable to recover the money from you. The contract requires you to hold the deposit as stakeholder; this means that you cannot use the money for your own purposes, other than as a deposit for your own purchase, thus reducing the risk to the buyer. A professional conveyancer will have insurance cover against loss or the deposit being misused, whereas you will not. It may be the case, therefore, that the buyer will not be happy about taking the risk of you holding the deposit. The buyer may suggest, therefore, that his or her conveyancer should hold the deposit on the terms set out in Standard Condition 2.2. This is perfectly acceptable (and safe) for both parties. However, if you intend using the deposit to fund the deposit on your own purchase, before agreeing to the change make sure that the buyer's conveyancer will cooperate in sending the money on to your own seller.

Insurance

Special Condition 5 in the contract (Special Condition 3 in the typed version) obliges the buyer to insure the house he or she is buying at the point of exchange. This is a reversal of the position laid down by the unamended Standard Conditions (that is, those which do not include any special conditions), which state that the seller bears any risk of damage between exchange and completion. So, under the Standard Conditions, if the house is damaged between exchange and completion, the buyer can withdraw from the purchase and you as seller would have to repay the deposit and would have no claim against the buyer. Special Condition 5 removes these rights from the buyer, so if the house is damaged, the buyer must still go ahead and complete and pay the full purchase price. He or she would then have to claim on his or her own insurance policy to pay for the damage.

The buyer may request that Special Condition 5 is deleted and the unamended Standard Conditions apply once more. This is not advantageous from the seller's point of view and it is not unusual for sellers to refuse to follow the Standard Conditions. However, consider your position carefully. It is likely that if you stick to your guns and insist that the Special Condition stays, the buyer will back down, but if it appears that he or she will not, you will have to decide whether to concede the point or run the risk of losing the sale. Obviously, the state of the property market may well influence both buyer and seller.

Chattels and stamp duty land tax

House sales often include carpets, curtains and other chattels (see page 56). An inclusive price for the house and chattels may have been agreed, or perhaps the buyer has agreed to pay, say, £2,000 extra for these. There is a space on the contract form for this separate figure to be included. Where chattels are included in the agreed price, the buyer may request that the inclusive price be apportioned on the form: so much for the house and so much for the chattels. This is a lawful device to save stamp duty. Duty is payable only on land, not on carpets and curtains. If an inclusive price is stated the duty is payable on the full amount. But if the price is apportioned, duty will not be payable on the part of the purchase price representing the chattels. There can be particularly large savings where the purchase price is just over £250,000. At a price of (say) £251,000, then £7,530 duty is payable; at a price of £250,000, only £2,500 duty is payable. If the buyer suggests this, you should agree to it, provided that the amount suggested in respect of the chattels reasonably represents their true value. There would be criminal penalties if, for example, the price was apportioned as £60,000 in respect of the carpets, and £1,000 in respect of the house! The amended figures should be inserted on the front page of the contract form.

Amendments to the contract

If it is necessary to amend the contract in any way, ask the buyer's conveyancer to suggest an appropriate form of words and to amend both copies of the contract manually. When the contract is signed, it will then be necessary for both parties to initial the alteration.

Queries on the title

The terms of the contract state that you as seller will accept no objections to the title, that is, your ownership of the house and the rights and obligations affecting it, but this condition is only binding on exchange; the buyer can still raise queries up to exchange.

However, it is unlikely that there will be any problems with the title. The Official Copy Entries set out clearly and precisely what you own and they are normally sufficient proof.

Other queries raised could be regarding any covenants or other occupiers of the property or land as described below.

Covenants

If there are missing covenants or existing breaches of the covenants affecting the property (see page 51), the buyer may request that you obtain insurance cover to protect against any potential breach. If this happens, check with the deeds (or the lender's conveyancer who is holding them), whether there is already such a policy in existence. If there is, the policy can be passed to the buyer on completion and he or she will gain its protection. If there is no existing insurance policy but the covenants in question are very old, there is no need for such cover as there is no risk to the buyer of the covenants being enforced.

However, if the buyer or his or her lender persists with this matter, you will need to decide whether to concede or not. This will depend on whether you want to risk losing the sale or how desperate the buyer is to buy. There is normally a single premium payable for defective title insurance, with a minimum of £200. It may be easier (and quicker) if you suggest that the buyer's conveyancer obtains quotes and takes out the insurance, and that the purchase price is then reduced by the amount of the premium. Alternatively, you can obtain the insurance yourself; there are several insurance companies with Internet sites who provide this form of insurance.

Occupiers

If the Preliminary Enquiries Form discloses that anyone other than the owners of the house is in occupation, for example a spouse, child or other relative, the buyer may want to make sure that any such person(s) will vacate the property on completion. If they do not, you as seller will be in breach of contract anyway as you have promised to sell with vacant possession. Still, the buyer may want written confirmation from the occupier(s) that they will leave, and if this is the case you will be able to send him or her a photocopy of the form signed by the occupier(s) that you should have already prepared (see page 60).

Signing the contract

When the buyer is ready to proceed, his or her conveyancer will return one copy of the contract to you, and retain the other copy to be signed by the buyer. It is important to make sure that the contract contains any agreed alterations – and none that have not been agreed – before you sign.

All the owners of the land should then sign in the box on the front page (at the end of the contract if you prepared your own form); there is no need for a witness. If there have been any alterations, you should also initial these. If there have been a large number of alterations, you may find it preferable to prepare, or 'engross', two fresh copies of the agreement, although this may delay matters as you will also need to send the new version to the buyer.

Preparing for exchange

Remember, once contracts have been exchanged it will be too late to change your mind and back out of the sale. So this is decision time; do you really want to commit yourself to selling this house?

Problems with chains

If you are involved in a dependent sale and purchase, you need to make sure that you exchange on both the sale and purchase as near simultaneously as possible. If you exchange on the sale and the purchase falls through at the last minute, you will have nowhere to live; you have sold your present home but have not agreed to buy a new one. If, on the other hand, you exchange on the purchase and the sale falls through, then you now have two houses, and you will probably not be able to afford to buy the new one if you were relying on the money from the sale. You will lose your deposit and run the risk of a substantial claim for damages for breach of contract.

Therefore, you must be ready to exchange on the purchase before proceeding – see the checklist opposite to make sure that all the necessary matters have been resolved and that you can safely exchange on the purchase.

Agreeing a completion date

When preparing for exchange, the first thing you must do is to agree a completion date with your buyer. It may be simpler to speak to the buyer personally, rather than negotiate through his or her conveyancer, but note that any date agreed directly with the buyer will be subject to confirmation from the conveyancer that the legal work can be done in time.

If you have a dependent sale and purchase you will need to arrange the same completion date for both the sale *and* purchase. This can be difficult and may involve numerous telephone calls before a date acceptable to both parties can be found. The people you are buying from or selling to may also be involved in similar dependent transactions, so a date will have to be agreed that is suitable for everybody else involved. This is quicker and simplified if you are doing your own conveyancing, as you will know immediately whether any date suggested is acceptable to you; a conveyancer acting on your behalf would need to get back to you before agreeing to a suggested date.

Exchange of contracts

The contract for the sale of land is drawn up in two identical copies – the seller signs one, the buyer the other – and is formed by the

---

Pre-exchange checklist

Before exchanging, check the following:

- have you (and any other owner of the house) signed the contract and initialled all alterations? (see page 69)
- have all other occupiers of the house signed a form to say that they will vacate on completion? (see page 60)
- have arrangements been made for the discharge of your existing mortgage? (see page 45)
- are all the financial arrangements in order? (see page 45)
- have arrangements been made for the payment of the deposit? (see page 66)
- have all outstanding queries been resolved, for example regarding fixtures or preliminary enquiries?
- in a sale and purchase, is everything ready for exchange on your purchase? (see page 116)
- has a completion date been agreed?
- has the same data been agreed on any dependent purchase?
- has the method of exchange been agreed with the buyer's conveyancer? (see page 70)

---

exchange of the two parts. The seller therefore ends up with the copy signed by the buyer, and the buyer gets the copy signed by the seller. This is one of the stages of the transaction where you will be at a slight disadvantage by not employing a conveyancer.

Conveyancers will normally 'exchange' contracts over the telephone. The contract is legally binding when this call is made. The two copies are physically exchanged later. This enables exchange to take place very quickly and is particularly convenient in the case of dependent sales and purchases – remember, you need to exchange on both transactions as close as possible to each other to avoid the problems of two houses or no house at all (see page 70).

Unfortunately, when acting on behalf of yourself, it will not be possible for you to exchange over the phone. Telephone exchange depends upon the fact that a conveyancer's verbal agreement to exchange will be enforced by the Law Society★, or the Council for Licensed Conveyancers★ should the need arise. There can be no such guarantee in the case of a private individual, should you break your word, for example, to send a deposit.

The procedure to be followed when exchanging contracts in the case of a purchase, and therefore also a dependent sale and purchase, is set out on pages 117–9.

If you are involved in only a sale, discuss with your buyer's conveyancer the procedure to be followed. This discussion should take place in advance of exchange. The buyer may well be in a dependent transaction and wish to exchange on both of his or her transactions swiftly. In this case, the best way to proceed is for you, in advance of exchange, to send your part of the contract to the buyer's conveyancer. You must make it clear that he or she is to hold this 'to my order, pending exchange'.

When the buyer is ready to exchange, he or she can advise you of this over the phone and you can then agree (assuming that you have not changed your mind) to 'release' the contract to him or her. The buyer's conveyancer should then agree to insert the agreed completion date in both parts of the contract, together with the date, and to send you the buyer's signed part of the contract together with the deposit cheque. You should make a contemporaneous note of the time and details of the telephone conversation – just in case! The buyer will then exchange by sending his or her part of the contract (and the deposit) to you through the post. The contract becomes legally binding when it is put in the post.

Insurance

Even though you have now agreed to sell the house, and the risk of any damage has passed to the buyer under the terms of the contract, you must not cancel your house contents or buildings insurance until completion. Although the risk of any damage passes to the buyer, it is safer to remain insured yourself, rather than have to make a claim against a buyer which has to be enforced by court action. In any event, if you have a mortgage on the house, it will be a term of the mortgage that you keep it insured.

You should now have successfully exchanged contracts for the sale of your house. The most difficult part of the work is now over and you can start preparing for completion – and moving.

Suggested letter to accompany the pre-contract package

Dear Sirs,

Your Client XXXX; purchase of 10 Coronation Street

I am the seller of the above property and enclose the pre-contract package consisting of:

- Draft contract (in duplicate)
- Fixtures and Contents Form (in duplicate)
- Preliminary Enquiries Form
- Official Copy Entries
- *[include copies of any guarantees etc. referred to in the Preliminary Enquiries Form]*

Please hold these documents to my order pending completion.

Please note that I shall be dealing with my own conveyancing work (although XYZ Conveyancers of .... *[insert name of lender's conveyancer]* will be dealing with the discharge of the existing registered charge).

I look forward to hearing from you as soon as possible that you approve the draft contract and with an indication of when you expect to be able to exchange. Please also advise whether the purchase is dependent upon the sale by your clients of an existing property and, if so, what stage that transaction has reached.

Yours faithfully,

Chapter 5

Selling your house – exchange to completion

On exchange of contracts a legally binding contract for the sale and purchase of the house now exists. Neither party can withdraw from the transaction without incurring legal liability.

Insurance

If the suggested amendments to Standard Condition 5 were included in the contract (see page 55), then the buyer now bears the risk of any damage to the house. However, you must not yet cancel your own insurance policy; it will be a term of your mortgage that you keep the house insured. Even if you do not have a mortgage, you must still not cancel your insurance policy. If there is damage to the house and the buyer breaks the contract and refuses to complete, without insurance you could be left with a damaged house and a worthless right to sue an impecunious buyer.

Estate agent

If you sold your house through an estate agent, you should now advise the agent that contracts have been exchanged. Also tell the estate agent what the agreed completion date is and ask for his or her bill. The estate agent's job is now over, and he or she will expect payment of all fees on completion.

Discharge of existing mortgages

You should also tell the lender's conveyancer of the agreed completion date and ask for a redemption figure for the repayment of the mortgage as of that date as soon as possible.

Discuss also the arrangements for completion. The lender's conveyancer will require that completion should take place at his or her offices, so ask for confirmation that he or she will agree to completion taking place by post. You should ask for confirmation (in writing) that he or she will give the buyer's conveyancer an 'undertaking' to discharge the mortgage and send the buyer's conveyancer Land Registry Form DS1 (see example in Appendix II) or to procure an Electronic Notification of Discharge of the loan. This is often referred to as an 'END'. Increasingly, lenders are notifying Land Registry that a loan has been discharged electronically, that is by email (the END), rather than using the paper DS1. The procedures for discharging mortgages are looked at in detail on page 80.

The Standard Conditions of Sale require that on completion the purchase price is paid by a direct transfer to a bank account. The money to discharge the mortgage must be paid by the buyer directly into the lender's conveyancer's bank account. The rest will be paid into your bank account. You will need details, therefore, of the conveyancer's bank account (name and number of the account, the name and address of the bank and the sort code), so that you can give these to the buyer. You will also need details of precisely how much will be required to pay off the mortgage calculated as at the date fixed for completion. Due to the fact that interest is payable on the loan, the amount due will change from day to day. You will often find, therefore, that when quoting the amount due on the day fixed for completion, you will also be given a 'daily rate', that is, an amount by which the figure quoted should be adjusted for every day after the agreed date that the money is sent. This is to cover the situation that completion might be delayed by a day or so and avoids having to obtain a further quote for the new completion day.

Also ask whether the lender's conveyancer will agree to act as your agent on completion, or whether it will be necessary for you to attend his or her offices on the day. It is likely that the conveyancer will want his or her fees paying on completion and you will need to be in a position to be able to hand over a cheque for the full amount (including VAT) on that day.

If you are involved in a dependent sale and purchase, you will also need to study the section on preparing for completion of the purchase on page 131.

The draft Transfer

The buyer must now draft the Transfer, the Land Registry document that will transfer the ownership of the house from you to the buyer. This is sometimes referred to as the 'purchase deed'. He

---

Checking the Transfer: Form TR1

Box 1 – Stamp Duty
The top part of this box used to be the space in which the payment of the duty was indicated. Following the introduction of stamp duty land tax, this box can now be ignored and left blank.

Box 2 – Title Number
This should be the same as that in the Official Copy Entries.

Box 3 – Property
This should be the full postal address (including postcode) of the property.

Box 4 – Date
This will be left blank and the date inserted when completion actually takes place.

Box 5 – Transferor
This should be the name(s) of all the owners of the house, as set out in the contract and the Official Copy Entries, i.e. your name ...

Box 6 – Transferee
This should be the buyer(s) name(s) as set out in the contract.

Box 7 – Transferee's intended address
This is of no concern to the seller, and should be left as drafted.

Box 8
This sets out the actual form of words which transfers the house to the buyer and should remain as printed on the form.

Box 9 – Consideration
The first box should have an X in it and the sentence 'The Transferor has received ...' should be completed with the correct amount of the purchase price, in words and figures. This should be the full amount payable for the house (i.e., not just the balance due on completion), but should exclude any amount specifically appropriated to chattels.

---

or she will send you two copies of the draft for your approval. You will need to make sure that it accurately reflects the terms of the contract – see box below. The Transfer should be completed on Land Registry Form TR1 – an example of this form is given in Appendix II.

Box 10 – Title Guarantee

An X should be inserted in the box alongside 'full title guarantee'.

Box 11 – Declaration of Trust

This should be left as drafted by the buyer; it is of no concern to the seller.

Box 12 – Additional Provisions – Do you need an Indemnity Covenant in your favour?

Look carefully at your copy of the Official Copy Entries to see if you entered into any covenants when you acquired the property. Look carefully at any covenants in the Charges Register; it will set out when they were entered into and who were the parties to that agreement. Was it you? If not, look then at the Proprietorship Register; is there a statement in it that you gave a 'personal covenant' when you acquired the property? If there are covenants in the Charges Register that were entered into before you bought the house, it is likely that you gave such a personal covenant when you bought.

If you entered into a covenant when you acquired the land, you will remain liable on that covenant even after you have sold the land. To protect yourself from being sued because the buyer, or any other future owner, breaks the covenant, you will need a covenant from the buyer that he or she will indemnify you if there is such a future breach. This will be the 'personal covenant' that you gave when you bought the house, a promise to the person you acquired the land from that you will indemnify him or her if there is a future breach of covenant.

Where you gave a covenant when you acquired the land, the buyer should have included this indemnity covenant in this box of the Transfer. This is required by Standard Condition 4.6.4. If the buyer has not included an indemnity, amend the Transfer by inserting one yourself. See page 125 for the correct form of words.

Box 13

This contains spaces for all the parties to sign and should include the names of all the parties to the Transfer.

Completion information

The buyer will normally send with the draft Transfer various enquiries about the arrangements for completion. You may not be able to answer all of these questions without the help of the conveyancer acting on behalf of your lender. There are various forms that conveyancers use for this purpose, but they will usually cover the following matters.

Property information

The buyer will require confirmation that all written information given by you before exchange still remains complete and accurate. If there have been any changes, for example fresh disputes with the neighbours, you should tell the buyer. However, provided that the information you originally gave was true, it will now be too late for the buyer to change his or her mind and withdraw from the transaction. If nothing has changed you should say so 'as far as you are aware'.

Vacant possession and arrangements for keys

You will also have to state what time on the day of completion you will have moved out and what arrangements are to be made for handing over the keys to the buyer. This is something you will need to consider carefully, bearing in mind that you do not want to agree to an arrangement that is too inconvenient for yourself.

The keys can be handed over personally by the seller to the buyer, but they are often left at the estate agent's office for collection. Occasionally they are handed over to the buyer's conveyancer at completion if this is convenient.

Completion

The buyers will wish to know where completion will take place. If you have a mortgage on the property, this will be the offices of the lender's conveyancer. The buyers will usually wish to complete through the post, but you will need to have ascertained from the lender's conveyancer if this is agreeable before you can answer this question.

If you do not have a mortgage on the property, then in theory completion can take place anywhere. However, bear in mind the practicalities of the situation and the convenience of the buyer as well as yourself. If the buyer's conveyancer is local, then it would be sensible for you to suggest that completion should take place at his or her office and that you will attend.

In other cases, you could suggest that completion takes place at the house, although any location other than a conveyancer's office will cause the buyer additional expense and inconvenience.

It is probably more sensible and most convenient for all parties to suggest to the buyer's conveyancer that, if he or she agrees to act as your agent (without payment), you will agree to completing at his or her offices, but without attending. You would need to send all the documentation through to the conveyancer in advance of completion, to be held 'to my order' (on your behalf) until the conveyancer sends the money through to your bank account.

Payment of the money due on completion

There will also be various questions relating to financial matters. Assuming that there is no delay in completion (see Chapter 9), all that will be due at this stage is the balance of the purchase price.

If there is no mortgage on the property you must now decide how you want the money to be paid. Under the Standard Conditions, the money can only be paid by a direct credit into a bank account using the banks' computerised money transfer systems. This method is more convenient and safer than using cheques or banker's drafts.

If you have an existing mortgage to pay off, the arrangement will be that the buyer pays over to the lender's conveyancer the amount required to pay off the mortgage and then pays what is left of the purchase price to you. You will therefore need to give the buyer details of your own and the lender's conveyancer's bank accounts (including the name and address of the banks, sort codes and the names and numbers of the accounts), so that the appropriate sums of money can be credited to them. You will have to tell the buyer's conveyancer the precise amount you wish to be sent to the lender's conveyancer's bank account to discharge the mortgage and the amount to be sent to your own bank account. This latter will be the balance due on completion, less the amount required to pay off the mortgage.

Discharge of existing mortgages

If you have one or more mortgages on the property, the buyer will ask for confirmation that these will be discharged on completion and for information as to who will give the undertaking to discharge them. Technically, the loans should be paid off before completion, and the buyer need not complete until this is so. However, to facilitate the transaction, the practice is for the buyer to pay the money over before the mortgage is paid off and to accept an 'undertaking' from the seller's conveyancer that the loan will be discharged.

An undertaking is a promise by a conveyancer to do something and is binding on that conveyancer under Law Society★ and Council for Licensed Conveyancers'★ rules. A non-conveyancer cannot give an acceptable undertaking as there is no guarantee and no sanction if the promise is not complied with. A buyer will therefore not give you the purchase money in return for a promise that you will pay off the mortgage. However, this situation is resolved by the involvement of the conveyancer acting for the lender. You should have already requested written confirmation that he or she will give an undertaking to the buyer to discharge the mortgage, and you can now pass on this confirmation to the buyer.

Signing the Transfer

When you have approved the draft Transfer, return one copy of it to the buyer. The buyer will now sign or 'execute' the Transfer and return it to you for signature. You should check that it has been properly signed and witnessed by all the buyers and then sign it yourself. You should keep the Transfer ready for completion, when it will be handed over to the buyer in return for the purchase price.

'Execution' consists of the seller and buyer (or all of them if there are more than one) signing the Transfer where indicated in the presence of a witness, who then also signs the document. In the case of two buyers or sellers, the same person need not witness both signatures. The date should be left blank until completion actually takes place.

Schedule of documents

If there is no mortgage on the property, you may have in your possession the Land Certificate (see page 37 regarding these no longer being issued after 13 October 2003) or the Title Information Document and probably the old title deeds (documents which prove the ownership of the land before the house was registered – do not throw them away). You will need to hand all the documentation you have with regard to the house over to the buyer and should prepare a 'schedule' (or list) of these documents in duplicate. When you hand the documents over to the buyer on completion, he or she should sign and return one copy of the schedule as a receipt for the deeds. Although strictly the Land Certificate (or Charge Certificate if there is a mortgage) is no longer required to be handed over to the buyer on completion, you will often find that it will be handed over. After all, the seller has no need for it.

If there is a mortgage on the property, the lender's conveyancer will deal with this.

Receipt for chattels

As explained on page 67, the purchase price may have been apportioned between the land and chattels, such as carpets and curtains. When paying over the purchase price on completion, the buyer will expect a receipt for his or her money. The Transfer Form (TR1) contains a receipt for money attributed to the land. But the money attributed to the chattels will need a separate receipt and you should draw this up now ready for completion. No special form of words is required; you can simply say 'Received from [name of buyer] the sum of £xx in respect of chattels at [address of property].' It should then be signed and dated.

Other preparations for completion

This book is concerned with the legal aspects of selling a house, but as a reminder the box on page 85 gives the practical steps that will need to be taken prior to completion.

If you are selling and buying a new house at the same time, you will need to study Chapter 7 carefully to ensure that you are ready to complete your purchase as well as your sale.

Finalising arrangements

If you will not be in attendance on completion, for example because the lender's conveyancer is acting as your agent, you will need to send the signed Transfer to the lender's conveyancer so that it arrives in good time for completion on the agreed date. Do not forget to include a cheque for the payment of the lender's conveyancer's fees. If a separate payment is made for chattels, you should also send a receipt for this. You must emphasise to the lender's conveyancer that these documents are to be held 'to my order' until you confirm that the part of the purchase monies due to you has been received in your bank account. Ask the conveyancer to phone you when he or she has received the monies to redeem the mortgage, and check that the balance of the purchase money has been credited to your bank account – only then can completion take place.

If the buyer's conveyancer is acting as your agent, similarly make sure that the signed Transfer and the Land Certificate, other title documents, the receipt for the chattels and two copies of the schedule of documents are sent to him or her in good time for completion. You must make sure that these are sent under the instruction 'hold to my order' until you have received confirmation from your bank that the purchase money has been received.

Do not forget to ask the conveyancer to sign and return one copy of the schedule as a receipt. Also, ask the buyer's conveyancer to phone you when he or she has instructed his or her bank to forward the money due to you on completion. It may take several hours, despite modern computer technology, for the money to reach your account and you should therefore make it clear to the conveyancer that you will phone back to confirm that completion can take place and the keys can be released to the buyer.

Completion

What happens on completion will, to some extent, depend upon which method of completion you choose. Generally, the buyer will pay over the balance of the purchase price and in return will receive the Transfer, Land or Charge Certificate – although these are no longer essential – and any other documentation relating to the house, and the keys. Completion will usually take place by post, but the keys will still need to be handed over either personally to the buyer or left at the estate agent's office for collection.

Where completion takes place by post, be careful not to hand over the keys to the buyer – and make sure the estate agent does not hand them over – until completion has taken place. Where there is a mortgage on the property, ask the lender's conveyancer to phone you when he or she has received the money to pay off the mortgage. Then check with your own bank that the balance of the money due for the house has been received. You can then get back to the conveyancer to confirm that completion can take place, and only then can you phone the estate agent and authorise the handing over of the keys. (Often, you will leave the keys with the estate agent only when you have received such confirmation – you may well still need to be in the house yourself to make all these phone calls.)

Where the buyer's conveyancer is acting as your agent, you will have sent him or her all the documentation to hold 'to your order' pending completion. You will have asked the conveyancer to advise you when he or she has authorised transfer of the money due. When you have received confirmation from your bank that it has arrived, phone the buyer's conveyancer to confirm this and that the various documents in his or her possession may be released to the buyer. If the estate agent has the keys, phone immediately to authorise their release to the buyer. If you still have the keys, take them to the agents or hand them over personally to the buyer.

Post-completion steps

Your legal work is now just about completed. There is little left for a seller to do once completion has taken place – unless you are using the money to buy a new house, in which case you will need to follow the advice given in Chapter 8.

Pay the estate agent
Advise the estate agent that completion has taken place and settle his or her bill as soon as possible.

Insurance
You can now cancel any buildings and contents insurance policies on the house.

Discharge of existing mortgage

This will be dealt with by the lender's conveyancer, and should be of no concern to you. However, you will need to cancel any standing order relating to the repayments on the loan.

Conveyancer's fees

You will need to settle the lender's conveyancer's fees, if you have not already done this prior to completion.

File your papers

Put away your file of papers in a safe place, in case any of them are needed again; you can then sit back and congratulate yourself on a job well done!

Timetable and checklist for moving house

About four weeks to one week beforehand
- Get 3 removal firms' estimates and/or quotes for D-I-Y van hire charges
- Having chosen a firm, confirm arrangements
- D-I-Y move: alert friends/family for help on the day (packing, driving, providing meals, cleaning up, being available)

Old address
- Arrange for meters to be read
- Arrange for disconnection of cooker, washing machine, dishwasher
- Arrange for carpet cleaning if required

New address
- Arrange for taking over gas, electricity
- Arrange for reconnection of cooker, washing machine, dishwasher
- Arrange for carpets to be laid

In general
- Tell telephone company when account to be closed
- Apply to take over telephone or request new telephone to be installed at new address and extra sockets if required
- Change-of-address cards – buy, or order printing (after new telephone number known)
- Arrange insurance of contents at new house from date of moving and during removal
- Start sorting and throwing things out, getting rid of surplus
- Arrange extra rubbish disposal
- Get boxes, packing material, strong string
- Buy stick-on labels
- Arrange hotel booking if required
- Ask relatives/friends to look after children
- Arrange for pets to be taken care of; book kennels if necessary

One week before
- Prepare diagram of new house with location of furniture

- Send off change-of-address cards
- Arrange for transfer of bank and building society accounts
- Apply to Post Office for redirection of mail

Old address
- Cancel deliveries and settle accounts for:
  – milk
  – newspapers

New address
- Arrange deliveries, e.g. milk

In general
- Put valuables and documents in bank/safe place
- Check arrangements for hiring van/borrowing car
- Get own car serviced, if necessary
- Confirm arrangements and timings for meter readings and disconnection/connection at old/new address:
  – electricity
  – gas
- Arrange with seller and buyer leave off/on:
  – electricity
  – water
  – heating
- Arrange to leave keys at old address
- Arrange collection of keys for new address
- Finish packing and labelling
- Prepare survival kit (see below)

Day before
- Pack personal overnight case(s)
- Organise meals/drinks for moving day
- Switch freezer to maximum (if moving it with contents)
- Take children to relatives or friends
- Deliver pets to kennels or elsewhere
- Get supply of cash (e.g. for tips, meals, petrol, coins for emergency telephone calls)
- Defrost refrigerator

Survival kit for moving day

- kettle/flex; teapot; tea/coffee; milk/sugar; disposable cups; teaspoons
- can opener; food; plates/cutlery; saucepan; camping stove if no cooker working
- washing up liquid/brush
- notepad/pens
- toilet paper
- any regularly taken medications and a first-aid kit including sticking plaster, scissors and aspirin
- cash; cheque book; bank cards; credit cards

- candles; matches; torch
- mobile phone or coins/phone card for public call box; telephone numbers of estate agent, solicitor, seller, your buyer, electricity and gas companies
- plugs; adaptors
- tool kit
- removal contract; driver's licence; motor insurance document
- a change of clothes; slippers; toiletries
- things to amuse children if they are with you

Chapter 6

Buying your house – finding a house to exchange of contracts

The first rule when doing your own conveyancing is to plan ahead. You should read through all of the parts of this book dealing with the purchase *before* you agree to buy a house and be sure that you understand what is involved in doing the work yourself. You will not have time once you have started the process to work out what happens at each stage; any delay means you are risking losing the house, or being in breach of contract and having to pay compensation to the seller.

You should buy all the forms you are likely to need during the transaction before putting your house on the market. Again, you will not have time to find and buy a particular form halfway through the transaction. See page 89 for a list of the forms required.

The longest part of the conveyancing process is the period from agreeing to buy a house and the contracts becoming legally binding. It is this delay that allows gazumping to occur, so anything you can do to reduce the length of time before exchange, the better.

Financial matters

There are some things you cannot do in advance of finding a house, such as the necessary searches (see page 105). However, if you need to arrange a loan to finance your purchase, it is wise to contact your preferred lender in advance of finding a property to make sure that it will lend you the amount you require. The lender will need to consider your creditworthiness before deciding whether to advance the money, as well as contact your employer and perhaps take up other references, and all this takes time.

Many lenders now issue a 'mortgage certificate' confirming that they will lend you up to a stated amount, subject to a suitable house being found. The lender will still need to undertake a valuation of the property you have decided on, but some time can be saved by getting agreement in principle in advance. The existence of a mortgage certificate may also help to make sure you get the house you have decided on – a seller faced with two prospective buyers may well opt for the one with finance already arranged.

There are various types of mortgage loans available and consideration of what may be best for you is beyond the scope of this book. However, you will find useful guidance as to the choice available in *Buy, Sell and Move House*, available from Which? Books★.

Lender's conveyancer

When you are applying for your loan, the lender will ask you to nominate a conveyancer to act on its behalf. This is usually the conveyancer that would be acting for you in the purchase. Where you are doing your own conveyancing, the lender will still need a conveyancer to act on its behalf. You can choose the conveyancer yourself (for example, one from whom you have obtained an acceptable quote for the work), or you could simply leave it to the lender to nominate a conveyancer.

How accessible are your savings?

If you intend to use some of your savings towards the purchase of the house, how much notice do you need to give the bank or building society in order to gain access to your money? If more than 30 days' notice is required, you should give notice now so that there will be no delay when you need to pay over the money.

Two or more buyers?

If there are two or more people buying the house or contributing financially towards its purchase, you will need to decide whether you are to own the house as 'joint tenants' or 'tenants in common'. In a joint tenancy, the financial interest of the owners is equal, and if one owner dies, the interest of the deceased passes automatically to the surviving owner(s). If you want the ownership to reflect the fact that one owner paid more towards the house than the other, for example A owns 40 per cent and B owns 60 per cent, then a tenancy in common is necessary. In this case, the deceased's share will be passed on according to his or her will in the usual way.

Where the co-owners are husband and wife, or partners in a long-term relationship, they will usually be joint tenants and happy for the interest of one to go automatically to the other if one of them should die. However, in the case of a second marriage, or where there are children from a previous relationship, you may wish to consider opting for a tenancy in common. Remember, with a joint tenancy the share of the deceased will automatically pass to the survivor; you cannot leave it by your will. If you want to leave your share of the house to your child (or anyone else for that matter), then you will need to be tenants in common.

However, you will need to think very carefully about all the implications of whatever decision you make. If you do decide to be tenants in common and then leave your share by will, this could make for difficulties after your death if your surviving partner wishes to continue living in the house and the child to whom you have left your half share wants the house to be sold.

This is not just a problem when you are doing your own conveyancing; you would have to make this decision if a conveyancer were acting for you.

If you opt for a tenancy in common, you will need to decide how you wish the share in the house to be split. This could be half each, or any share you like – for example, to reflect the amount each contributed to the purchase of the house. This will need to be stated in the Transfer (see page 124).

It is possible to convert a joint tenancy into a tenancy in common after you have bought the house. This can be simply done by giving a written notice to the other co-owner, stating 'I sever my joint tenancy of … [description of house]'. In this case, you will end up owning the house half each, no matter what contribution each made to the purchase. This is another consideration to bear in mind when deciding how you will own the house, particularly when one person is contributing more to the purchase than the other. They are, in effect, making a gift of the extra amount they have contributed to the other.

Buying the forms

You will need the following forms:

- LLC1 – Local Land Charges Search (one copy)
- CON29 – Enquiries of Local Authority (two copies)
- CON29DW – Enquiries of Water Authority (two copies)
- K16 – Application for Official Search (Bankruptcy Only) (one copy)
- Land Registry Form AP1 – Application to Change the Register (one copy)
- Land Registry Form OS1 – Application for Official Search of the Whole of the Land (one copy)
- Land Registry Form TR1 – Transfer of Whole of Registered Title (three copies)
- SDLT 1 – Land Transaction Return (one copy)

Depending upon the area in which your new house is situated, you may need to carry out additional searches for which additional forms will be required, and you should read page 105 below before buying your forms.

Although only a few copies of the forms are required, you may find it advisable to obtain some 'spares' just in case there is a problem completing them. You may also find that you are unable to buy just one copy of a particular form as they are often sold in packs of five.

Where to buy the forms

Legal forms will be available from a law stationers; look in the *Yellow Pages* for a local firm. Alternatively, Oyez Straker* offers an on-line and a telephone ordering service for the forms. Land Registry forms AP1 and TR1 can also be downloaded free of charge from Land Registry's website at *www.landreg.gov.uk*. Note, however, that SDLT 1 is only obtainable direct from the Inland Revenue*. Each form has a unique reference number, so photocopies will not be acceptable. When contacting the Inland Revenue to obtain the form ask also for a copy of the guidance notes, which will explain in detail how to complete the form.

When you have found a house to buy

The remainder of this chapter assumes that you have found a house you like and your offer has been accepted by the seller. Helpful tips on all aspects of finding a house, dealing with estate agents and so on are covered in *Buy, Sell and Move House,* available from Which? Books*.

At this stage you should bear in mind that the longer the delay before you are in a position to exchange contracts, the greater the risk of gazumping, and you will need to attend quickly to the following matters.

Arranging finance

Now that you have decided on the property you wish to buy, contact your lender to obtain a formal offer of a loan. As mentioned earlier, there are various checks that the lender must carry out before an offer of a mortgage can be made, such as contacting your employer for confirmation that you will be able to fund the repayments, and these can be done before you have found the house you want to buy. However, once you have found a house the lender will also need to commission a valuation of the property to make sure that it will be adequate security for the loan. You will be expected to pay for this valuation, and not all lenders will allow you to see the valuer's report even though you are paying for it.

Valuation or survey?

When you are arranging for the valuation, the lender may ask whether you also require a structural survey of the house. The valuation commissioned by the lender is only a statement of the value of the house, and although the value will to some extent depend upon the structural state of the house, the valuer will not undertake a detailed survey of the structure. He or she cannot be held responsible for failing to point out structural defects, unless, perhaps, the defects are particularly obvious.

It is always advisable when buying a house to have some kind of structural survey of the property. A house is, after all, the biggest investment most people will make in their lifetime, and you should therefore make sure it is structurally sound. The problem, of course, is the cost; a full survey can cost upwards of £500, depending upon the value of the house. You should at the very least, however, get a Home Buyer's Report. This is a report on the structure of the house in a standardised form, which is somewhat cheaper than a full survey but should show up most problems. If you arrange for this report through your lender, it will take the place of the valuation report and so you will save the fee for that.

Depending upon their lending criteria, lenders will only advance a certain percentage of the value of the house, and often the maximum is 90 per cent. Some will lend over 80 per cent of the value only if you pay an additional fee, such as a mortgage indemnity guarantee, or a high-lending fee (this usually takes the form of a single lump-sum payment), or agree to a higher rate of interest resulting in higher monthly repayments. Either way, consider very carefully whether you can afford to buy the house, taking into account not only the monthly repayments, but also whether you will have enough cash on the day of completion to meet the full purchase price. Think also of the impact an increase in interest rates might have on you in the future. At the time of writing, interest rates are at a very low level; any change is likely to be upwards and this will quickly result in higher mortgage payments. Could you afford to make increased payments if and when interest rates rise? Do not overstretch yourself financially.

Can you afford to buy the house?

You will need to ensure that you have sufficient funds with which to buy the house. In addition to the actual purchase price you will need to consider the following.

Deposit

It is usual for a buyer to be expected to pay 10 per cent of the purchase price as a deposit on exchange of contracts. Note that when doing your own conveyancing you may not be able to use the deposit received on the sale of your existing house (see page 117), and if you do not have sufficient savings you will not be able to fund the deposit on your new house.

If you intend to use some of your savings for the deposit, remember that you may have to give the bank or building society notice in order to get access to your money. If you have not already done so, give notice now so that the money will be available when you need it.

If you are only a few thousand pounds short of the required 10 per cent, you may be able to persuade the seller to accept a reduced deposit, but you cannot rely on this.

If it is purely the case that you will have the funds on completion, but are just short of the ready cash on exchange, then you could consider a bridging loan. This is a short-term loan from your bank or building society to 'bridge the gap' between when you need the money (that is, exchange) and when you will have the funds (that is, on completion). However, bridging loans can be costly. On top of the interest for the period of the loan, the lender will also charge an arrangement fee, which could be several hundred pounds. If you think a bridging loan may be necessary, find out well in advance what the cost is likely to be and make sure that you can still afford to go ahead with the purchase (see below). Also take care to find out how much notice the lender will require for the funds to be made available to you.

Stamp duty land tax

This is a government tax payable by the buyer of a house. It used to be called stamp duty because a stamp was placed on the deed to show that the duty had been paid. As of 1 December 2003 stamp duty was replaced by stamp duty land tax which is payable (at the same rates) on most property transactions, but without the deed actually having a stamp placed on it. Instead, you will receive a certificate to prove that you have paid it. The amount of duty varies according to the value of the house. The rates currently payable are as follows:

- value up to and including £60,000 – no duty payable
- value from £60,001 and up to and including £250,000 – duty payable at 1 per cent of purchase price
- value from £250,001 and up to and including £500,000 – duty payable at 3 per cent of purchase price
- value exceeding £500,000 – duty is payable at 4 per cent of purchase price.

Duty is payable on the whole of the purchase price; so where a property has a value of £100,000, duty of 1 per cent is payable on that sum, so you will have £1,000 stamp duty land tax to pay. Note that stamp duty land tax is probably going to be your largest expense in buying a new house.

Some duty can be saved where the sale is to include carpets and curtains, or other chattels (see page 67). Duty is not payable on chattels, only on land, so if the price can be apportioned as to so much for the land and so much for the chattels, rather than having an inclusive price for both, duty will only be payable on the amount apportioned to the house and not on that apportioned to the chattels.

Although this saving will normally be small, a larger saving can be made where the price is just over one of the price bands that determine the rate of duty. So if the price for house and carpets is £61,000, duty of £610 is payable. If the price is apportioned as £60,000 for the house and £1,000 for the carpets, no duty will be payable, as the amount now being paid for the house does not exceed the threshold at which duty becomes payable. Note, however, that the amount allocated to the carpets (or other chattels) must be a fair representation of their actual value. It would be fraud to allocate an unreasonably large sum to the chattels; for example, you would not be able to apportion an inclusive price of £270,000 as £20,000 for the carpets in order to avoid the £250,000 jump in rates of duty – unless, of course, the carpets are really worth that amount!

Note also that if the house you are buying is in a 'disadvantaged area', as defined by the government, no duty is payable unless the price exceeds £150,000. Disadvantaged areas are basically those suffering from an element of social deprivation, but due to the way the areas are mapped, when you are buying a house for £150,000 or less, it is always worthwhile checking whether your property is in such an area. This can be checked on the Inland Revenue's website*.

Land Registry fees

A fee will have to be paid to Land Registry for registering you as the owner of the land. The rates depend upon the price you are paying for the house (again, excluding chattels). The current fees are shown in the table overleaf.

Land Registry fees

Value (£)	Fee (£)
0–50,000	40
50,001–80,000	60
80,001–100,000	100
100,001–200,000	150
200,001–500,000	250
500,001–1,000,000	450
1,000,001 and over	750

You can find out about any amendments to Land Registry fees by phoning any Land Registry Office (see Appendix I), or from Land Registry's website at *www.landreg.gov.uk*.

Search fees
When buying a house there are various searches and enquiries you will need to make of the local authority and other public bodies (see page 105 for more information on searches), and you will have to pay for these. Which searches you need to make, and thus the total cost, will depend upon the location of the house, but you should allow between £200 and £250 for these.

Lender's valuation fee/cost of survey
Whether you are buying a house with the aid of a loan or not, a survey is always advisable. If you commission a full structural survey, this will cost from around £500, depending upon the value of the property. A Home Buyer's Report may cost from around £250, again depending upon the value.

Cost of forms
If you are doing your own conveyancing, you will have to buy any of the necessary forms yourself. Although these are quite cheap, you may find difficulty in obtaining single copies so the total cost could be as much as £40.

Bank charges
You will have to pay your bank or building society a fee for transferring the money to the seller on completion. The seller will not

accept a cheque, so you will need to use either a banker's draft or (more often) send the money direct to the seller's bank account using the banks' computerised payment systems. The fee for either will vary from company to company and may depend upon your relationship with the bank/building society, but can be as much as £40.

Lender's conveyancer's fees

Where you are financing the purchase with the aid of a loan from a bank or building society, the lender will require a conveyancer to act on its behalf with regard to the transaction. You will have to pay that conveyancer's fees, and you will need to budget around £200 for this.

Contacting the seller's conveyancer

Your estate agent will give you the name and details of the seller's conveyancer (if no agents are involved in the sale, ask the seller for these details). You should then write to that conveyancer, telling him or her that you will be handling your own conveyancing, and requesting the 'usual pre-contract package' as soon as possible. Tell the conveyancer your position with regard to financing the purchase, that is, whether it is a cash purchase or dependent on a loan or selling your existing house. If you are relying on a loan or the proceeds of a sale, the seller's conveyancer will need to know what stage these arrangements have reached, for example that the loan has been agreed in principle, subject to a satisfactory survey; or that a buyer has been found for your existing house. You should then find out whether the seller's sale is dependent upon him or her finding another house, and if so what stage that transaction has reached. (You will probably have discussed all these details with the seller and/or the estate agent prior to your offer being accepted, but it is as well to get the details in writing.)

The pre-contract package

The seller's conveyancer will send to you a package of documents and information setting out the details of the seller's property and the terms of the sale (the pre-contract package). As a minimum it will include the draft contract for sale and Official Copy Entries of the register of title to the property. There will also probably be a Property Information Form containing information about the house and a Fixtures, Fittings and Contents Form setting out what is and is not included in the sale. Remember, the seller is only under an obligation to tell you of any legal problems affecting the land or its ownership, for example that it is subject to a covenant restricting its use. He or she need not reveal details of the new motorway about to be built at the bottom of the garden, for example, or about the nasty smell from the neighbouring animal by-products factory, and it is largely up to you, as buyer, to find out any information about the property that may influence your decision to buy.

In addition to studying this pre-contract package, therefore, you will need to make various pre-contract searches and enquiries to find out as much as you can about the house (the need for a survey to find out about any structural defects has been covered earlier in this chapter). And if you find out now something about the house or surrounding area that you do not like, you can walk away without any liability to the seller. But if you find out something untoward after you have exchanged contracts, it will then be too late to change your mind – you will be legally committed to buy and will not be able to withdraw from the purchase.

Which searches and enquiries you need to make will depend upon the situation of the house, and the most common are set out below. If you are buying with the aid of a mortgage, contact the conveyancer acting for the lender to tell him or her which searches you intend to make and ask whether the lender will require you to make any additional searches (see below). The lender will be concerned to see the results of all your searches, as the security of the loan will depend upon the saleability of the house.

Contents of the pre-contract package

The pre-contract package will always contain:

- the draft contract
- the Official Copy Entries and plan.

And may also contain:

- the Fixtures, Fittings and Contents Form
- the Property Information Form (PIF)
- a copy of planning consents and/or guarantees relating to the property.

Approving the draft contract

The contract sets out terms on which the seller is prepared to sell the house to you. It is likely that the seller will be using a contract incorporating the Standard Conditions of Sale. These are a set of terms governing the sale drafted by the Law Society★ in an attempt to standardise the small print used in conveyancing contracts. Sometimes the contract will actually set out the Standard Conditions in full, or simply state that they apply without listing them all. Either is perfectly in order. A copy of the Standard Conditions can be found in Appendix II. Check the contract for the following.

Seller

Check that the name of the seller is the same as that indicated in the Proprietorship Register of the Official Copy Entries (see page 38). If two or more people are registered as proprietors, then all must be named as parties to the sale. If there is any discrepancy, you should take this up with the seller immediately and ask for an explanation. The only acceptable explanation for a person so named not being party to the sale is when he or she has died. If this is the case, you will need to see a copy of the death certificate – ask the seller for this. Consider also the advice given later on in this chapter in the section 'Investigating title' (see pages 109–14).

Buyer

Check that your full name and address is inserted as 'Buyer'. If you are buying the house jointly with another person (or more than one other person), make sure that the names and addresses of *all* buyers are included.

Property

Make sure that the land is stated to be freehold; you can confirm this by looking in the Property Register of the Official Copy Entries. Remember, if the house is leasehold, you will not be able to do your own conveyancing. Check also that the description of the land in the contract (particularly the postal address of the house) ties in with that in the Property Register – the contract gives details of what the seller is agreeing to sell to you, and the Official Copy Entries what the seller owns, so the two should be the same. Note, however, that there will be some things included in the Register which do not need to be included in the contract, for example reference to a plan of the property.

If the contract states that you are buying only part of the land included in the Property Register, complex legal issues arise – you will not be able to proceed with your own conveyancing and must seek professional advice.

Root of title/title number

Root of title refers only to unregistered land and should be deleted (remember, you will only be able to do your own conveyancing if the property is registered). Check that the title number stated is the same as that in the Official Copy Entries supplied. If no title number is given here, with reference to a conveyance instead, then the land is unregistered and you will not be able to continue with your own conveyancing. You must consult a conveyancer.

Incumbrances

Incumbrances should be checked very carefully. This part of the contract lists the obligations to which you will be legally bound if you decide to buy the house. Make sure there are none included which in any way might prevent or restrict your use of the house.

The contract does not usually list the incumbrances in detail, but will instead refer to the entries on the Register, for example 'The Property is sold subject to the covenants contained or referred to in entry number 1 on the Charges Register'. You should check that the entries referred to do not include any 'Registered Charges' – these are mortgages, and you should expect to buy free from them. If any are included as incumbrances, check with the seller that it is in order to amend the draft contract to exclude them. You do not want to buy land subject to existing mortgages.

Make sure you understand what the incumbrances are. If you buy the house, you will be bound by any incumbrances and there may be court action against you if you breach them in any way. If the covenants on the Register were entered into many years previously, you may find the wording in the Official Copy Entries old-fashioned and difficult to understand. However, with the help of a good dictionary, you should be able to work out under what obligations they place you.

Common covenants are: to use the house only as a 'dwelling-house', that is, for residential purposes only; not to build on the land or extend a property until a named person's consent has been obtained; and not to cause a nuisance or annoyance. A fuller explanation of incumbrances is given in the section 'Investigating title', later in this chapter (see pages 109–14).

Title guarantee

This is a guarantee by the seller of his or her ownership of the land, and that it is not affected by any incumbrances other than those mentioned. The seller should normally give full title guarantee. If the seller is offering only limited guarantee, ask the seller's conveyancer to change this to a full title guarantee. However, if this request is refused, there is no point in arguing at length over this matter; most conveyancers take the view that title guarantee is not of any great importance with regard to registered land as Land Registry's own guarantee of ownership can be relied upon.

Completion date

This should be left blank. It will be agreed and inserted into the contract on exchange.

Contract rate

If either party is unable to complete on time, he or she must pay compensation to the other. This consists of the payment of interest on the purchase price at the 'contract rate'. If it is left blank, the Standard Conditions will imply that the Law Society★ interest rate will apply. This is 4 per cent above the Barclays Bank base rate. Alternatively, the seller can insert his or her own interest rate. Check that this is not excessively high – 4 or 5 per cent above the base rate of a UK clearing bank is acceptable, but anything higher than this should be resisted. However, if the seller refuses to reduce the rate, you should not let this affect your decision to buy, as it is only relevant if there is a delay in completion.

Purchase price

You should check that the price stated on the contract is the same as agreed between you and the seller. Check also that the amount payable for chattels is correct and that the balance due on completion has been calculated correctly.

Special Conditions

On the reverse of the Standard Conditions contract form there is space to incorporate what are known as Special Conditions. These allow the seller to vary the Standard Conditions to meet the needs of the particular transaction. Check these carefully. The following are common.

- A provision stating that in case of any conflict between this contract and the Standard Conditions, the provisions of this contract will apply. This is usual and causes no concern.
- A provision preventing the buyer raising any requisitions or objections with regard to the title. This is usual, and will prevent you as the buyer questioning matters relating to the title after exchange. It is essential, therefore, that if there are any queries you wish to raise, you do so before exchange (see page 109).
- A provision stating that vacant possession will be given on completion; if the contract does not include this, contact the seller's conveyancer and ask that it be added. If he or she is not agreeable to this, do not buy the house.
- A provision requiring you as buyer to enter into an indemnity covenant with regard to the covenants affecting the house. This is a usual provision and there is no need for you to be concerned about it. In certain circumstances, a seller can still be held liable for a breach of the covenants even after selling the land. To protect against this, the seller will require you to enter into this covenant that you will perform the covenants already affecting the house and indemnify, that is, compensate, the seller if he or she suffers loss because you have not complied with them. As long as you comply with the covenants, you have nothing to fear from this provision.
- A provision excluding Standard Conditions 5.1.1 and 5.2.1 (under Standard Condition 5, if the property is damaged between exchange and completion, for example by fire, this is the seller's responsibility), or stating that the 'risk' is to pass to the buyer on exchange. Indeed, under this condition, the buyer can withdraw from the transaction if the property is severely damaged. Many sellers consider this provision unacceptable and exclude the condition by this type of Special Condition. This means, therefore, that as a buyer you will need to make

sure that you insure the house as soon as contracts have been exchanged, so that if the house is damaged, although you will still have to buy it, you can claim on the policy.

Fixtures, Fittings and Contents Form

This form lists those items that are included in, or excluded from, the sale, such as light fittings, curtain rails and so on. In practice, more disputes than in any other area of the transaction occur when one party assumes particular items are included in the sale and the other party assumes that they are excluded. Therefore, check this form carefully to make sure that you are satisfied with its contents. If items are being removed which you expected to be included in the sale, for example the garden shed, contact the seller to renegotiate.

Seller's Property Information Form (PIF)

It is likely that the seller will provide a Property Information Form containing the answers to various questions regarding the house. If the form is not provided, see 'Preliminary enquiries of the seller', on page 109.

The form is in two parts. Part 1 consists of the seller's answers to a series of questions about the property. Part II consists of the seller's conveyancer's answers to similar questions.

Study the answers carefully. The seller is not legally obliged to answer all the questions (though most sellers do), but where he or she does so, the obligation is to answer them truthfully, and you as buyer are entitled to rely on them when deciding whether or not to buy the house. If the seller's answer to a particular question proves subsequently to be incorrect, you may have rights to claim compensation from the seller or, in an extreme case, even withdraw from the purchase.

Pay particular attention to the answers regarding the following.

Boundaries
Who maintains which fence may be of interest to you as buyer, but more important is whether any boundary has been moved within the last 20 years; if so, this could lead to disputes with a neighbour as to ownership.

Disputes with neighbours

If there have been, or are still, disputes with neighbours, do you really want to buy yourself into what may be a 'neighbours from hell' situation? Look carefully at the cause of the dispute and assume the worst, that is, that the neighbour is in the right. Do you still want to buy?

Notices

Any notices received must be thoroughly investigated; they could affect your enjoyment of the property or your legal rights.

Guarantees

Make sure any guarantees are handed over to you on completion. National House Building Council (NHBC) and Foundation 15 documentation are particularly important – if you are buying a house built within the last ten years, you must ensure that you obtain one or the other of these guarantees as to the structural soundness of the house. Do not buy without one or the other. The NHBC* guarantee provides a ten-year guarantee against structural defects, and Foundation 15 a similar 15-year guarantee.

Services

Check whether any of the services (for example gas, electricity and water) serving the property pass through a neighbour's land or are shared with a neighbour. If they pass through a neighbour's land, you will need a legal right, an 'easement', for them to do so. Check whether such a right is included in the Official Copy Entries. If not, find out how long the rights have been enjoyed. As long as they have been enjoyed for 20 years or more without any objection, there is no need to worry. If they have been enjoyed for a shorter period, there is a danger that the use of the neighbour's land for any of these purposes could be prevented. Although you may be prepared to take such a risk, your lender may not be – discuss matters with your lender's conveyancer.

If your services do run across a neighbour's land or are shared in some way, there should be proper arrangements as to their repair and maintenance. Note that there is no provision for creating these arrangements if they are not already in place and so when the services need repairing there may be disputes as to who is liable to do or to pay for the work. Again, you may be prepared to accept this, but your lender's conveyancer may not.

Access

Most houses can be accessed directly from the public highway and so there is no problem. But sometimes the only access is across land belonging to someone else, maybe a 'private' road. Be very careful to ascertain whether there is anyone else's land between the house and the public road. If you need to cross this to get to and from the house, you will need a legal right (an easement) to do so. This should have been granted when the house was built and should then be set out in the Property Register. If there is no such right on the Register, enquire of the seller whether there is any documentary evidence of such an easement being granted – it might just not have been entered on the Register. If there is no such right, it is possible to acquire a right by long use. If the access has been freely used for 20 years or more, then the law will presume the grant of a right of access on foot.

Arrangements and rights

The question of arrangements and rights asks about informal arrangements affecting the house, such as a neighbour having an informal agreement to take a short cut across the land. Informal arrangements can be converted by the law into formal, legally binding arrangements; if any arrangements are revealed, do not buy the house unless you are agreeable to being subject to any right stated. Even if you are agreeable, your lender might not be and could refuse the loan.

Occupiers

If the form reveals that anyone else other than the registered proprietor(s) (and their infant children) is in occupation, insist that the additional occupier(s) signs an agreement that he or she will leave the property prior to completion (see page 60 in Chapter 4 for an example of this kind of agreement). Although the seller is under an obligation to give you vacant possession, it is better to have confirmation from any other occupier(s) that they will leave, rather than risk them still being there at completion and you being unable to move in.

Building work

Building work on the property may have required planning permission. If the answers with regard to the question of building work reveal that work has been carried out within the last four years, is it important to make sure that planning permission was obtained, or that it was unnecessary, and you can confirm this with the planning authority (usually the district or unitary council). If planning permission was required for the work, but none was sought by the seller, then the planning authority can serve an enforcement notice requiring that the building be demolished, and there are criminal sanctions for non-compliance. However, if the work was carried out more than four years ago, it is immune from this enforcement.

You should also ensure that Building Regulation consent was obtained for any building work. This is in addition to planning permission and is to ensure that the building work was carried out to the correct standards and using proper materials. You should insist on receiving evidence of consent no matter how long ago the work was carried out. If this is not available, you should require the seller to obtain insurance to cover you against possible enforcement proceedings that could be brought by the local authority.

Check the Official Copy Entries to see if there are any covenants on the property that prohibit building work or require consent to be obtained. Even if planning permission was obtained, the covenant must still also be complied with. If there is evidence of non-compliance with the covenant, ask the seller to obtain consent under the covenant now, or request that he or she obtains insurance to cover the problem (see page 114 for details of this).

Changes of use

In the unlikely event that there have been any changes in the use of the property within the last ten years, planning permission will again be required. However, it is usually the case that the property is, and always has been, used solely for residential purposes.

Which searches should you make?

There are certain searches that will need to be made in all cases, and others that depend upon the location of the property. If you are buying with a mortgage loan, you should at an early stage be in touch with the lender's conveyancer regarding which searches you intend to make, and ask whether the conveyancer wishes you to make any others.

The following searches should be made for every purchase.

Local land charges search

Local authorities are bound by statute to keep a register, open to public inspection, of various matters affecting property in their area. The local Land Charges Register is searched by submitting Form LLC1 to the Local Land Charges Department of the district, London borough or unitary council for the area in which the house is situated. Check the address of this department in the telephone directory or phone the council's enquiry desk. A personal search can also be made at the council offices, but this is not recommended other than for experienced conveyancers, and will not be acceptable to the lender's conveyancer. See 'Enquiries of the local authority', on page 106, for details of the fee for this search.

Completion of the Form LLC1 is simple. You will need to fill in:

- the name and address of the local authority
- in the 'Requisition for Search' box, make sure you request a search of the whole Register by deleting 'Part(s)... of'.
- in the 'Description of the Land' box, insert the full postal address of the property you are buying.

This will normally be sufficient, but in the case of properties that cannot be readily identified from their postal address, a plan may be necessary. Do not forget to include your own name and address for the return of the search.

The search will give a summary of anything affecting the house. Further details of entries can be obtained by visiting the council offices to inspect the documents yourself, in which case the following might be revealed:

- **tree preservation orders (TPOs)** – these prevent the tree in question being felled or lopped without the permission of the local authority
- **smoke control orders** – these prevent the burning of non-smokeless fuels in domestic fireplaces
- **compulsory purchase orders** – this is where local and national government, or other public bodies, have statutory

powers to acquire land compulsorily in certain circumstances. If such an order affects the land you are thinking of buying, you will be bound to sell to these bodies and there will be no guarantee that the price you will receive will be more than, or even the same as, the price you are now paying. It is therefore best to look for an alternative property

- **planning charges** – if there are any Enforcement Notices, Stop Notices, Closing Orders or Light Obstruction Notices registered against the property, you should not proceed further with the purchase without taking legal advice. The Register might also indicate that there are conditions attached to planning permissions. This is not unusual. You should ask for details of the conditions, if they have not been supplied, and make sure they have been complied with. If they have not, you will need legal advice before proceeding

- **financial charges** – in certain situations, the local authority can charge the payment of money it has spent on, for example, making up private roads, to the owners of the houses benefiting from that work. If you see any financial charge registered against the house, whether for roadworks or anything else, write to the seller asking for confirmation that the charge will be removed on or before completion. If confirmation is not forthcoming, you are probably best advised not to buy the house, as the responsibility for this type of payment would fall to you. However, if the seller is prepared to reduce the purchase price by an amount equivalent to the amount of the charge, you might find this acceptable.

Enquiries of the local authority

These are submitted to the same local authority and at the same time as the local land charges search. They consist of a series of questions about the house on form CON29.

The appropriate form should be submitted in duplicate together with the fee. One cheque will cover the fee for both the local search and the enquiries of the local authority. However, there is no standard fee for these enquiries, as each local authority sets its own charges. You will, therefore, need to phone the local land charges department of the appropriate council to find out what it charges. The combined fee is likely to be between £100 and £200. You will also need to consider whether you need to make any of the additional enquiries (see below); if so, ask how much the additional fee for these will be.

Insert the description of the property on the front page of the form; if the house fronts on to more than one road (for example, it is a corner plot), also insert the name of the other road at the bottom of the 'Description of Property' box. Part I of the form comprises the enquiries for all cases; the Part II enquiries will be answered only if the appropriate box on the front page alongside the number is ticked and an extra fee paid. You should consider making the additional enquiry 5 (to see if the property has a public right of way over it).

Following is a description of various searches that may need to be made in certain cases.

Coal mining search

If the property is situated in what is or was once a coal mining area, you will need to carry out a coal mining search to find out whether the property is likely to be affected by subsidence from past, present or proposed coal mining activities. Following the privatisation of the coal industry, the search is made on Form CON29M and submitted to the Coal Authority★. A plan showing the location of the property will be required. Contact the Coal Authority for information on the fees for this type of search. You can ascertain from the Coal Authority's website whether your house is in an area where such a search is needed, and then conduct the search on-line rather than using a paper form. Remember that coal mining was not just confined to the North of England – there used to be coal mines in parts of Kent and Somerset, for example!

Other mining searches

If you are buying a house in certain parts of Cheshire, you will need to carry out a search to make sure that the land is not liable to subsidence caused by salt mining. Similarly, when buying in west Devon or Cornwall, the land may be affected by china clay or tin mining. These searches are made by letter to the Cheshire Brine Subsidence Compensation Board★, English China Clay/Imerys★ and Cornwall Consultants★ respectively, and will usually need to be accompanied by a plan showing the location of the property.

Railway lines

If the house you are buying adjoins a railway line, you will need to contact Network Rail to find out, for example, who owns the fences and what rights Network Rail has to enter your land for maintenance. The search is made with the Network Rail Area Surveyor. A plan will be required and a fee is payable. It has to be said, however, that due to the current state of the rail industry following Railtrack's collapse this search may not reveal anything useful.

Canals, rivers, streams

If a canal, river and so on flows through or alongside your land, you will need to make a search with the Environment Agency★. This will reveal the ownership of the river bank, fishing rights and so on. A plan will be required and a fee is payable.

Commons Registration Search

Common rights are the rights of the inhabitants of an area to use a piece of land in a particular way. Often these rights are of ancient origin but will include rights of way or grazing. Make this search if you are buying land that has not previously been built upon or where it adjoins a village green or other common land. The search is made in duplicate on Form CR21, which should be submitted to the county or unitary council. Contact your county council for details of the fee payable.

Environmental matters

Concern about the environment has significantly increased in recent years. It is sensible when buying a house, therefore, to consider whether it is affected by any environmental problems. One way of doing this is to commission a 'Home Envirosearch'. This is a reasonably priced (£39) search of a database compiled by the Landmark Information Group★, which gives information on environmental matters such as radon gas, landfill sites and so on. More information and a sample report can be obtained from Landmark's website at *www.landmark-information.co.uk*. The search itself is available from Jordans Ltd★. The Environment Agency also offers an on-line environmental report – currently priced at £47 – at *www.environment-agency.gov.uk/*.

Other information

It is wise to obtain as much information as possible about the area in which your new house is situated before committing yourself to buying it. Several Internet sites may be of interest to prospective house buyers – for example, *www.upmystreet.com* gives a wide range of information gathered together from official statistics. By typing in your postcode you can find out, for example, information about local schools, council tax, crime statistics and police clear-up rates. The Environment Agency also offers a free 'What's in Your Backyard Pollution Inventory', giving details of harmful factory emissions in your area. Note, however, that these sites do not give information of a legal nature.

Preliminary enquiries of the seller

If the seller does not provide you with a Property Information Form (PIF) as part of his or her pre-contract package, you will need to send him or her a Preliminary Enquiries Form (see pages 62–3 in Chapter 4) to complete, and you will need to study the replies carefully.

Investigating title

When investigating title you are concerned to check that the seller is indeed able to sell the property and to ascertain the incumbrances or third party rights affecting it (see page 31). You will do this in two ways.

Inspection of the house

Look around the property carefully for evidence of any third party rights affecting the land. Check whether there are any worn paths or tracks across the land, gaps in hedges or fences, which might indicate the existence of a right of way. Also check whether anyone other than the seller is in occupation of the land. If you discover any other occupiers, or rights of way affecting the land, these should have been revealed by the seller in the Property Information Form, or in the Preliminary Enquiries Form (see above). If they have not been disclosed to you by the seller, contact the seller's conveyancer and ask for clarification. See page 112 for what to do about any problems.

Checking the Official Copy Entries

An example set of Official Copy Entries is given in Appendix II. Check the following:

- that the Copies are up-to-date. Land Registry will not accept a search to update Official Copy Entries dated more than 12 months ago. If the Copies are already more than 12 months old – or are likely to be so by the time you are due to complete – then you should insist on the seller providing up-to-date Copies
- that the description of the property in the Property Register is the same as that in the contract. Note that if the seller is selling only part of the land he or she owns, you will not be able to do your own conveyancing
- the Property Register may also contain details of easements benefiting the land. These are likely to be prefixed by the words 'Together With'. If the property is subject to certain easements, that is, rights that others have over your land, these are likely to be prefixed in the Property Register by the words 'Subject to' or 'Except and Reserved'. Consider these rights carefully as they will be binding on you when you buy the house. However, it is not unusual for houses to be subject to rights for the neighbours' pipes, cables and so on to pass under your land, and unless you are planning any building work on the land, these should not concern you. If you are planning building work, such as an extension, the existence of easements such as these will restrict where you can build. You cannot build if doing so interferes with these rights in any way, even if you obtain planning permission
- that the names of the proprietors in the Proprietorship Register are the same as those given as the sellers in the contract; if X, Y and Z own the land, all three must participate in the sale of it. If one of the co-owners has died, see page 114 as to whether you can continue to act for yourself or whether you need legal advice
- that there are no restrictions or cautions on the Proprietorship Register (see page 38). If there are any restrictions other than those listed as acceptable in Chapter 3, you should seek legal advice before proceeding

- whether the Official Copy Entries include reference to a personal covenant. This is not necessarily a problem, but as explained on page 38, you will need to give a similar covenant when you buy
- that the Charges Register sets out the third party rights binding upon the property.

You are entitled to expect that any Registered Charges will be paid off by the seller (however, to check that the sale is not subject to these see 'Incumbrances', on page 98). But other easements or covenants included will be binding upon you when you buy the land and you will need to ensure that you understand what burdens will affect you if you go ahead and buy the house.

Easements can also appear in the Property Register (see above). Covenants are very common, so make sure that there are no covenants that have already been broken, or which your proposed use of the land might break. It is common to find a covenant that prevents building without the consent of a particular person. If there has been any building on the land, check that the appropriate consent was obtained. If there is no mention of consent on the seller's Property Information Form, ask the seller for evidence, or an explanation as to why he or she alleges that consent was not required.

Many covenants will have been entered into decades ago – sometimes over a hundred years ago. But they could still be enforceable and you cannot afford to ignore them even if they do now seem out of date, as you will risk being sued. Most covenants will not cause a problem, however, particularly if the house is to be used for residential purposes only. If you intend to use the house for business as well, you will probably be best advised not to buy if there is a covenant against using the land for this purpose. How to deal with problems with covenants is covered below.

Dealing with title problems

There are not usually any problems with the title as presented by the seller. If you are uncertain of anything with regard to the title, write to the seller's conveyancer for clarification. Try to make sure that you include all your questions in one letter – nothing will annoy the seller's conveyancer more than a constant stream of letters. You should also include any questions from the lender's conveyancer.

Following are a number of common problems.

- **Existing breaches of covenant** If you are not going to continue with whatever is causing the breach, there is no problem, and you can ignore it. So if there is a covenant not to use for business purposes and the seller has broken this, this can be ignored if you are not going to use the house for business purposes. But if you intend carrying on the breach, or continue using a building built in breach of a covenant, you could be sued, even though you did not initiate the breach. If there is an existing breach, and you are buying with the aid of a mortgage loan, let the lender's conveyancer have full details of the problem. You might like the house so much that you are prepared to take the risk of being sued, but the lender will not want to take any risk. Ask the lender whether it will require that indemnity insurance be taken out, and, if so, on what terms (see page 114 for details of indemnity insurance).

  It is unlikely that this type of insurance will be available where a breach is recent, and the lender will not be prepared to lend the money on the house. If the breach originated more than 20 years ago, the lender may be prepared to proceed without the need for any insurance. If you are buying without the aid of a mortgage loan, you should require the seller to take out indemnity insurance anyway.

- **Proposed breaches of covenant** These are situations where your intended use of the property will breach a covenant. Often, this will mean that you will have to look for another house; however, if the covenant is old, for example it was entered into 50 or more years ago, it may be possible to take out indemnity insurance. Generally, the more recent the covenant, the less likely it is that insurance will be available. Make sure your lender's conveyancer is happy with the terms of any policy offered to you.

- **Missing covenants** Details of any old covenants may have been lost over the years. These covenants will still be binding on you, even though you do not know what they are. Again, you will need to find out the requirements of the lender's conveyancer in such a situation. Indemnity insurance in relation to such covenants is usually available – indeed the seller may already have obtained such insurance – but you must make sure that the lender is satisfied as to the terms of the policy offered.

In the case of very old covenants where the house has been established on the land for many years and you do not intend to change the use of the land in any way, a conveyancer may take the view that there is no risk from any missing covenants and insurance is therefore not necessary. However, where you are buying with the aid of a mortgage you must obtain prior agreement to this from the lender's conveyancer.

- **Easements affecting the land** If you discover, from your inspection, any easements affecting the land not previously disclosed to you by the seller, ask the seller for details. Consider carefully whether any easements (whether disclosed or not) will affect or interfere with your proposed use of the house. If the property is subject to a right of way, there is little you can do about it. In theory you could ask the person with the benefit if they would agree to discontinue using it – but their reaction will be either 'NO', or 'how much is it worth to you'? The only practical solution would be not to buy – and remember that at this stage you are not legally committed to buy and so can withdraw without any legal comebacks. Remember also, that if the easements are anything other than the usual ones regarding pipes and drains, they could affect the saleability of the house, so even if you are prepared to proceed and put up with the inconvenience, you will need to check with the lender's conveyancer whether you will still be able to borrow the amount originally agreed.

- **Changes of name** You may find that one of the sellers has changed his or her name since buying the property, for example the house may be registered in a woman's maiden name which she has subsequently changed on marriage. You will need documentary proof of the change of name, such as a copy of the marriage certificate, or a copy of the deed by which the name change was effected. This documentary proof can be obtained from the seller's conveyancer, and must be forwarded to Land Registry when you apply for registration.

- **Death of a co-owner** If one of more than two co-owners has died, you can buy from the survivors, provided that at least two are still alive, but you will need the death certificate of the deceased. If one of two co-owners has died, and there is a restriction on the Proprietorship Register (see pages 34–5), you will not be able to do your own conveyancing. If there is no Restriction, then you can safely buy from the survivor, provided you obtain the death certificate of the deceased. However, if the sole proprietor of the house has died and you are buying from his or her personal representative (executor or administrator), you will not be able to do your own conveyancing.

Indemnity insurance

If there are title problems – and particularly problems with covenants – it may be possible to take out insurance to cover the risks involved, so that if you are sued for breach of covenant, the insurance company pays out to compensate you for any damages you have to pay. This insurance is widely available, provided the risk of being sued is fairly slight. If you are buying with the aid of a mortgage, you will need to discuss with the lender's conveyancer whether insurance will be acceptable as a solution where there are title problems.

A single, one-off premium (minimum £200) will be payable and this will depend upon the risk involved and the value of the property.

If insurance is necessary as a result of the seller's breach of covenant, once you have a quote for the cost of the insurance try to negotiate with the seller that he or she pays this cost. However, note that this is not always possible in a seller's market.

Dealing with the lender's conveyancer

The lender's conveyancer will be as concerned as you are with regard to the title and searches. The lender will wish to ensure that should it need to sell the house to recover the loan it will be able to do so. You should therefore make sure that the lender's requirements are complied with before you commit to purchase.

Send a copy of the Official Copy Entries, the Property Information Form, replies to any queries you have raised with the seller and the replies to your searches to the lender's conveyancer, and ask whether the replies are satisfactory or whether there are any matters requiring further clarification. If you have done your work correctly there should be nothing else that the lender requires you to do – except in the case of matters mentioned above where you are advising of particular problems. Note, though, that you cannot expect to use the lender's conveyancer as a source of free legal advice. You chose to do your own conveyancing and must do so – or pay extra for the advice.

Signing the contract

Once you have approved the draft contract, and any queries you and the lender's conveyancer may have with regard to the title, the Property Information Form or your searches have been resolved, return one copy of the contract to the seller, stating that it has been agreed 'as drawn', where there are no amendments, and that it is agreed 'as amended' if there are. Make sure that any agreed amendments have been incorporated into both copies. You, along with any other buyers, should then sign in the box provided. There is no need for a witness. **Do not date the contract or insert a completion date.**

The deposit

Unless you are in a dependent sale and purchase (see page 117), you will need a banker's draft for the payment of the deposit; the seller will not accept a private cheque. Your bank or building society will need sufficient cleared funds in your account before it will issue a draft, so make sure that the money has been paid in and has cleared in ample time for exchange. Find out from your bank or building society how much notice it requires to issue a draft once the funds have cleared – this could be as much as 24 hours' notice. If you are using a bridging loan from the bank or building society, you should already have arranged this and ascertained how much notice will be required for the money to be made available to you. Alternatively, you could arrange for your bank to send the money directly from your bank account into the seller's conveyancer's bank account. Obviously in that case you will need details of that bank account.

Exchanging contracts

You will have to consider the mechanics of how you are going to carry out exchange of contracts.

Pre-exchange checklist

Before exchanging contracts, you must ensure that you are ready to exchange. Once you have exchanged contracts it will be too late to change your mind. Do not exchange on either your sale or your purchase until you are satisfied with the following matters.

- Are the terms of the contract acceptable to you?
- Are you sure that the incumbrances on the property will not cause you any problems with regard to your proposed use of it?
- Have any title or other problems been resolved to your satisfaction and to the satisfaction of your lender's conveyancer?
- Have you made all the necessary searches?
- Have you received replies to all the searches?
- Have any problems arising from the replies been dealt with to your satisfaction and to the satisfaction of the lender's conveyancer?
- Do you have the money to pay the deposit?
- Have you obtained quotes for insuring the house from exchange, if this is necessary?
- Have you received the results of your survey, and are they satisfactory?
- Have you double-checked your finances to ensure that you can afford the transaction?
- Have you received your mortgage offer?
- Have you discussed with the seller's conveyancers the arrangements to be followed for exchange?
- Are you clear what you will have to do to effect exchange?
- Do you really want to buy this house?

Purchase only

If there is no linked sale this will be very straightforward. When you are ready to exchange (see 'Pre-exchange checklist' above) telephone the seller's conveyancer to see if the seller is ready. If so, agree a completion date. You can then either exchange contracts in person at the conveyancer's office, or send your part of the signed contract (and the banker's draft for the deposit) by post to the seller's conveyancer. The seller will then post his or her part back to you and the contract comes into existence the moment the seller's part is put into the post.

Dependent sale and purchase

If you are involved in a dependent sale and purchase, there are more complications. You will need to exchange on both sale *and* purchase. Remember, as there is not yet a binding contract, either buyer or seller can withdraw at any time – and people frequently back out at the last minute. The danger is that you exchange on your sale and then find that your purchase falls through, leaving you with nowhere to live. You cannot get out of your contract to sell just because your purchase has fallen through. Another danger is that you exchange on your purchase and then find that the sale falls through for some reason. Now you have two houses, and it is likely that you will not be able to afford to buy the new house as you were relying on the money from the sale of your existing house.

Conveyancers avoid these problems by exchanging contracts over the telephone. Contracts are not exchanged until assurance has been given that all parties to the contract are ready to exchange as well. The conveyancer will then exchange on the sale over the telephone and then as soon as possible thereafter exchange on the purchase in the same way, eliminating the risk.

Unfortunately, if you are doing your own conveyancing, you will not be able to exchange over the phone. Telephone exchange depends upon the use of conveyancers' 'undertakings' (promises given by conveyancers that will be enforced by the Law Society*, or the Council for Licensed Conveyancers* should the need arise), and there is no similar mechanism covering non-conveyancers to ensure compliance with any agreements entered into over the phone. This also means that you will not be able to use the deposit received on your sale towards the deposit on your purchase unless your buyer's conveyancer will send the money direct to your own seller.

However, when doing your own conveyancing you can use a combination of postal and telephone exchanges in order to make sure that you exchange on both transactions. Discuss with the conveyancers acting for both your buyer and your seller the procedure you wish to follow for exchanging contracts in advance of exchange.

The best way to proceed is to send your part of the contract for your sale to the buyer's conveyancer in advance of exchange, making it clear that he or she is to hold the contract 'to my order, pending exchange'. At the same time, send your contract for your purchase to your seller's conveyancer, together with the banker's draft for the deposit. Again, make it clear that you are sending these to be held to your order, pending exchange.

Next, agree a convenient completion date with the person you are buying from and the person you are selling to. Remember, you need to agree the same day for both your sale and your purchase, unless you are willing to move into temporary accommodation between the sale of your present house and buying the new one. You cannot arrange a date for your purchase prior to the date for the completion of your sale as you will probably need the proceeds from your sale in order to buy the new house.

Once the completion date has been agreed, you can exchange. You should exchange on your sale first, but before you do, contact the conveyancer acting for the person you are buying from explaining that you are ready to exchange and ask for confirmation that he or she will exchange with you later in the day to make sure, as far as possible, that you do not exchange on your sale only to find that your seller has changed his or her mind.

Next, phone the conveyancer acting for your buyer and, assuming he or she is ready to exchange, agree to release the contract by way of exchange, in return for an undertaking from the buyer's conveyancer that the contracts are exchanged as at that moment and that the buyer's part of the contract will be put in the post to you that night. The conveyancer should agree to insert the date and the agreed completion date into both parts of the contract. If, as is likely, it has been agreed that the conveyancer will hold the deposit, you will also want an undertaking that the buyer's deposit has been received. Make a note of the conversation and what was agreed, and the name of the person you spoke to at the buyer's conveyancer, just in case something goes wrong.

Having now exchanged on your sale, immediately phone the conveyancer acting for the seller of the house you are buying and adopt a similar procedure. Release your part of the contract and the deposit to the conveyancer in return for an undertaking that the contracts are treated as exchanged as at that moment. You will also require the conveyancer to undertake to insert the date and the agreed completion date in both parts of the contract and to put the seller's part of the contract in the post to you that night. Again, make a note of what was agreed and the identity of the person with whom it was agreed.

Conclusion

Having successfully exchanged, the vast bulk of your legal work is now over. You are committed to buy the property and it is now too late to change your mind. Remember, if the 'risk' of damage to the property passes to you (see page 100), you should immediately arrange to insure the house as from the day of exchange (see Chapter 7).

Buying your house – exchange to completion

You are now committed to buying the house; unless the seller is at fault in some way, you cannot now change your mind and decide not to buy. If you attempt to do so, you will be in breach of contract; at the very least you will lose the deposit you have paid, and may have to pay substantial additional damages to the seller.

Insurance

Depending upon the terms of the contract, you may need to insure the house as from the point of exchange. If the Standard Conditions of Sale were used by the seller without any amendment with regard to insurance (see page 100), then the risk of any damage to the house before completion remains with the seller; for example, if the house is damaged by fire, the seller is under a contractual obligation under Standard Condition 5 to restore the house to the condition it was in at exchange. If the damage is so bad that the house is unusable, you as buyer have the option to withdraw from the contract and claim back your deposit. However, you will have no additional claims against the seller.

The Standard Conditions are often modified by the deletion of Standard Condition 5, and a Special Condition is sometimes added to the effect that the buyer is to bear the risk of damage to the house after exchange (see page 100). In either case, the risk will now pass to you. If the house is damaged after exchange, you will still have to proceed with the purchase and pay the full purchase price.

To protect against having to pay for a pile of ashes, it is essential that you insure the house as soon as exchange takes place. If you are buying the house with the aid of a loan, the lender will also be concerned that the property is insured and may have offered to organise the insurance for you when you arranged the loan. If you accept the offer, telephone the lender to ensure the insurance takes effect from exchange. If you have decided to arrange your own insurance, do so quickly over the phone (you should have obtained quotes for this prior to exchange).

Protecting the contract

Although the seller is now legally committed to sell to you, there is always a risk that he or she will break the contract and sell to someone else. Although you have the right to sue the seller for breach of contract in such a case, this would involve lengthy and costly legal proceedings, and you would have lost the house anyway.

However, it is possible to put an entry on the Land Register to protect your contract. If the seller did sell the land to someone else, this entry would force the person to whom it was sold to sell it to you on the same terms as you had agreed to buy it. In reality, this prevents any breach-of-contract sale taking place, as no one is likely to want to buy the house only to have to resell it to you.

It is not usual, however, in an ordinary conveyancing transaction for the contract to be protected. Completion usually takes place only a comparatively short time after exchange and the chances of the seller selling to someone else during that period are therefore very slight. But where there is to be a lengthy delay before completion (for example, over a month), consider registering the contract at Land Registry. This can be done by completing Land Registry Form UN1 (which can be downloaded from the Internet – see page 89) and sending it to the appropriate Land Registry Office with the appropriate fee, details of which can be obtained from Land Registry website★ or the local office by phone.

Money

If you are using your savings to fund part of your purchase, do not forget to give the necessary notice to your bank or building society to withdraw the money so that it is available ready for completion. You should also allow sufficient time for any cheque to clear once it has been paid into your bank account, or you will not be able to draw against it.

Advising the lender's conveyancer

You should inform the conveyancer acting for the lender of the date fixed for completion as soon as you know when this will be. Ask the conveyancer for the mortgage deed for signature as soon as possible so that you can execute and return it before the date fixed for completion. Also discuss the arrangements for completion. It will be necessary for the lender's conveyancer to obtain the mortgage loan from the lender in order to hand it over directly to the seller. You will then have to hand over the balance of the purchase price, whether this is from your savings or from the proceeds of the sale of your present house. Once you have found out from the seller the arrangements proposed for completion (see page 127), pass this information on to the lender's conveyancer at once. In the meantime, however, you can ask for confirmation that the lender's conveyancer will deal with stamping and registration matters after completion, subject to your providing the completed forms necessary for this and (of course) paying the necessary fees. You will need to hand over cheques for the requisite amounts on completion.

Tell the conveyancer that you will make the 'usual pre-completion OS1 search and bankruptcy searches on behalf of the lender' and request confirmation that this is acceptable. Some lenders' conveyancers will prefer to do these searches themselves, but most will expect you to provide them.

Drafting the Transfer

Next, you will need to draft the Transfer. This is the deed that transfers the ownership of the land from the seller to yourself, and it is drafted on Land Registry Form TR1 (see Appendix II). Two copies of this form will need to be sent to the seller and one copy should be sent to the lender's conveyancer. The form should be completed as shown in the box below.

Completing Form TR1

Box 1 – Stamp Duty
This can now be ignored. It was required for the old system of stamp duty but is no longer needed for the new system of stamp duty land tax.

Box 2 – Title Number
Insert the number as it appears in the Official Copy Entries.

Box 3 – Property
Insert the full postal address (including postcode) of the property.

Box 4 – Date
This should be left blank and the date inserted when completion actually takes place.

Box 5 – Transferor
Put in the name(s) of all the owners of the house, as set out in the contract and the Official Copy Entries.

Box 6 – Transferee
This is where you insert your name. If you are buying with someone else, then the names of all the buyers should be inserted.

Box 7 – Transferee's Intended Address
In this box you will put the address where you will be living after you have bought the house (this will usually be the address of the house you are buying); this will then be entered on the Register. It is important that it is completed correctly, as any official correspondence regarding the house will be sent to this address. It is possible to state up to three addresses for service, one of which must be a postal address – but not necessarily within the UK. You can also use an email address. But do think very carefully about using overseas addresses – the Registry may need to send you important notices about the house which must be responded to within defined time limits. These will not be extended where an overseas address is used. If you do change your address, it is essential that you change the address for service on the Register so that you do not miss any notices that may be sent to you.

Box 8
This sets out the form of words which transfers the house to the buyer and should remain as printed on the form.

Box 9 – Consideration

Place an X in the first box. The sentence 'The Transferor has received ...' should then be completed by inserting the purchase price, in words and figures. This should be the full amount payable for the house (that is, not just the balance due on completion), but should exclude any amount for chattels.

Box 10 – Title Guarantee

Place an X in the box alongside 'full title guarantee', or 'limited title guarantee', depending upon which was stated in the contract.

Box 11 – Declaration of Trust

You should complete this only if you are buying the house with another person(s). If you have decided to own the land as joint tenants, you should place an X in the first box. If you have decided on being tenants in common in equal shares, you should place an X in the second box. If you have decided to own the land as tenants in common in unequal shares, you will need to place an X in the third box and then complete the sentence setting out the agreed shares, for example: *'The transferees are to hold the property on trust as to one third for [insert full name] and as to two thirds for [insert full name]'*. These different methods of ownership are considered more fully in Chapter 6.

Box 12 – Additional Provisions

Look carefully at your copy of the Official Copy Entries to see if the seller entered into any covenants when he or she acquired the property. Look especially carefully at any covenants in the Charges Register, which will contain details of when they were entered into and who were the parties to the agreement. Was it the seller? If not, look then at the Proprietorship Register; is there a statement in this Register that the seller gave a 'personal covenant' when he or she acquired the property (page 38 shows you what this looks like).

If the seller entered into a covenant when he or she acquired the land, he or she will remain liable on that covenant even when the land is sold. To protect him- or herself from being sued because you as buyer, or any other future owner, breaks the covenant, the seller will need a covenant from you that you will indemnify him or her if there is such a future breach. This is required by the terms of the contract. The seller will sometimes have added a Special Condition to the contract that an indemnity is required; if not, the indemnity will be required by Standard Condition 4.6.4 anyway. It is likely that an indemnity will be required in most cases, and it should be inserted into this box using the following words:

'The Transferee covenants to indemnify the Transferor against liability for any future breach of the covenants contained or mentioned in the Charges Register and to perform them from now on.'

If there is more than one buyer, the following form of words should be used:

'The Transferees jointly and individually covenant to indemnify the Transferor against liability for any future breach of the covenants contained or mentioned in the Charges Register and to perform them from now on.'

This form of words means that the seller can sue the buyers together or individually, should the need arise.

You are the Transferee and the seller is the Transferor. This covenant is a standard provision in a conveyancing transaction and should not cause a problem, provided you comply with the covenants.

Box 13

This provides a space for the transferor/seller to sign. The buyer does not always need to sign the deed. If the buyer is entering into a covenant, or there is more than one person named as buyer, the buyer will need to sign also. A separate clause should be inserted for each person as follows (this is sometimes already printed on the form):

Signed as a deed by

[insert name]

....

in the presence of

(Signature of witness)   ....

(Name of witness)   ....

(Address of witness)   ....

....

....

The draft Transfer will now need to be sent in duplicate to the seller's conveyancer (also keep a copy for your own files), and at the same time you should send your enquiries regarding the arrangements for completion (see below), again in duplicate and retain a further copy for yourself.

Request for completion information

You will need to ask the seller the following questions about the arrangements for completion. You can do so by letter, or in a form as shown in the box below. You will need three copies of the form – two to go to the seller's conveyancer and one copy for your own files.

Request for information about completion

Property:
Seller: *[Complete details]*
Buyer:

QUESTIONS

1. **Keys**
   Please confirm that ALL keys will be handed over on completion. What arrangements are to be made for the handing over of the keys?

2. **Completion**
   Where is completion to take place?
   Are you agreeable to completion taking place through the post?
   Will you act as my agent on completion?

3. **Vacant possession**
   By what time of day will the sellers have vacated the property?

4. **Money**
   Please advise as to the exact amount payable on completion. If this is not just the balance of the purchase price, supply a statement showing how this sum is calculated.

Replies to the Completion Information Form

When you receive the replies to the Completion Information Form, inform the lender's conveyancer of the arrangements proposed for completion as soon as possible – the easiest way to do this is to send a photocopy of the form, as the lender will also need to know the details of the seller's conveyancer's bank account.

Check in particular the reply to Question 5 regarding mortgages. It is essential that an undertaking is given with regard to the discharge of **all** the mortgages on the property before you buy it. (This undertaking is a promise by the conveyancer that he or she will pay off the mortgage and send you Form DS1 as proof of this. It is usual to rely on such undertakings in a conveyancing transaction.) If such an undertaking is given on the Completion Information Form in response to Question 5, it will take effect as

---

On completion the money will be paid direct into your bank account, please supply the following details:

- Bank name and address
- Sort code
- Your account number and name.

5. Mortgages

Please confirm you will give the usual undertaking to discharge all existing mortgages on the property and to send form DS1 as soon as received by you.

Your confirmation of this will take effect as such an undertaking on payment to you of the purchase price.

Please also confirm that you will give a similar undertaking to the buyer's mortgagee's conveyancer, if required.

6. Property information

Please confirm that, as far as you and the seller are aware, all information given in writing by or on behalf of the seller prior to exchange of contracts continues to be complete and accurate.

ANSWERS

(Leave a full page here for the conveyancer's replies)

---

soon as you pay the purchase price. However, the seller's conveyancer may prefer to give you a separate undertaking on completion. This is perfectly acceptable, provided that the conveyancer promises now that he or she will give you an undertaking on completion, and of course that one is given. The conveyancer may reply that the lender in question makes use of Land Registry's system of Electronic Notification of Discharge (END for short). It is equally acceptable for the seller's conveyancer to undertake to arrange for the lender to send the END to Land Registry.

Pre-completion searches

You will need to make two further searches about a week before the date fixed for completion (see below). This ensures that there is enough time for the replies to be made, and also enables you to send the results to the lender's conveyancer prior to completion. Do not make these searches more than about ten days prior to completion as the post-completion work of paying stamp duty land tax and registering the transaction at Land Registry has to be done within 30 working days of the search being made.

Land Registry search

Land Registry Form OS1 (see Appendix II for an example form) is used for this search, and should be sent to the Land Registry Office for the area in which the property you are buying is situated (this will be stated on the Official Copy Entries – see Appendix I for the address). A cheque for the £4 fee should be made payable to Land Registry.

Completing the first part of the form is quite straightforward. You should complete the first box with the details of the Land Registry Office where the title is registered. You can obtain the name of the Office from the Official Copy Entries – see Appendix I for the address. The remainder of the form consists of 12 numbered boxes and should be completed as follows.

- **Box 1** – Insert the administrative area and so on, which can be found in the property register on the Official Copy Entries.
- **Box 2** – Insert the title number – again to be found on the Official Copy Entries.

- **Box 3** – Place an X in the first box – the fee is currently £4.
- **Box 4** – Insert your own name and address.
- **Box 5** – The lender's conveyancer may require the search to be sent directly to him or her, in which case insert his or her name and address. Otherwise, leave blank.
- **Box 6** – Insert the full names of all the proprietors as set out in the Proprietorship Register as shown on the Official Copy Entries.
- **Box 7** – **This is very important.** Insert the date shown on the Official Copy Entries as being the day on which the copies show the Register. If you get this date wrong, then you may find yourself subject to entries on the Register of which you are unaware. Insert the date stated at the top of the Official Copy Entries; this date should never be more than 12 months old, as the Registry will not search for a period longer than this.
- **Box 8** – **Again great care is needed here.** If you are buying without the aid of a mortgage loan, it will be the name(s) of the buyer – or all the buyers if more than one. If you are buying with the aid of a mortgage it will be the name of the mortgage lender and **not** your name. This is to avoid the need for a separate search to be made on the lender's behalf. Such a search will protect you also. (If your lender's conveyancer has indicated that he or she will be doing a search on the lender's behalf, complete this box with your own name.)
- **Box 9** – If you are buying with the aid of a mortgage, place an X in Box C. If you are buying without a loan (or if the lender's conveyancer will be making a search on the lender's behalf), place an X in box P.
- **Box 10** – Insert the address of the property as shown on the Official Copy Entries.
- **Box 11** – Place an X in the first box (Registered Land Search).
- **Box 12** – Simply sign and date in the usual way.

Bankruptcy search

A search will also need to be made to make sure that you and any co-buyers are not bankrupt. It is necessary to provide the lender's conveyancer with an official search form as proof of this.

This search is made on Form K16, completion of which is simple. In the section headed 'Names to be searched', insert **your** full name and the full names of any other buyers. A separate line should be used for each name to be searched. Next, complete the box giving details of the applicant's name and address (in this case, your own). Ignore any references to 'Key Number'. The search form, together with a cheque for £2 per name you would like to be searched, should be sent to the Land Charges Registry★ Searches Department.

Return of searches

The results of both of these searches should come back by return of post. The bankruptcy search should state 'No subsisting entries'. However, if the search reveals a bankruptcy entry against someone with the same name as you, but living at a different address, you will need to contact the lender's conveyancer immediately to advise him or her of the entry, and that it does not refer to you – any delay could result in the mortgage funds not being available on completion, and a consequential action by the seller for breach of contract. Ask also what proof of this the lender's conveyancer will require. You may need to make a statutory declaration that you are not the person revealed by the search and do not and have never lived at the address in question. A statutory declaration is a written statement that you declare to be true in the presence of a conveyancer.

The Land Registry search should indicate that no further entries have been made on the Register since the date of the Official Copy Entries. If there are new entries on the Register, contact the seller's conveyancer and insist that the entries are removed. You have not agreed to buy subject to these entries and the seller will be in breach of contract if he or she fails to remove them. Also inform the lender's conveyancer of any entries revealed and ensure that he or she is agreeable to any remedial steps proposed by the seller.

Execution of deeds

The Transfer and the mortgage deed (if any) will need to be executed (that is, signed and witnessed) in ample time for completion.

The mortgage deed will be drafted by the lender's conveyancer and sent to you for execution. It should be signed by all the persons named in the contract as buyers of the land. Each buyer should sign the deed in the presence of a witness, who should also then sign and print his or her name and address. The same witness need not witness all the signatures. The mortgage deed should then be sent back to the lender's conveyancer, but make a photocopy before doing so, as this will be required by Land Registry.

As already mentioned, the buyer does not always need to execute the Transfer. If execution is necessary, once the draft has been approved by the seller, it will be sent back to you. If no amendments were necessary, your draft can now become the document to be signed by the parties. If amendments have been made, you should draw up another copy of the Transfer incorporating the agreed amendments. However, if there are only minor amendments it is possible to make the changes by hand, although you must make sure that the alteration is initialled by all parties when the Transfer is executed. The Transfer should then be signed and witnessed in the same way as the mortgage deed, and sent back to the seller's conveyancer as soon as possible, as the conveyancer will need time to arrange for the seller to execute the deed prior to the date fixed for completion. It will then be handed over on completion, duly executed by the seller, in return for the balance of the purchase price.

If it is not necessary for the buyer to execute the Transfer, the seller's conveyancer will retain the draft (assuming that no alterations are necessary) and obtain the seller's execution ready for completion.

Preparing for completion

Completion normally takes place by post. However, the Completion Information Form will include details of the completion venue, and you may wish to attend personally in order to see the culmination of all your efforts. Completion usually takes place at the seller's conveyancer's offices, or occasionally at the office of the seller's lender's conveyancer and this may be too far for you to travel, particularly as you will be organising your move.

Under the Standard Conditions, the money due on completion has to be sent by a direct transfer from your bank account (or the account of your lender's conveyancer if you are buying with the aid of a mortgage loan) into the account of the seller's conveyancer. You will need to ensure that you have sufficient cleared funds in your bank account on the day so that there will be no problem with the transfer. Check with your bank or building society how much notice it will require to transfer the funds in this way. A fee will be charged by the bank for this service.

Stamping and registration forms

Immediately after completion you will need to deal with the stamping and registration of the transaction. Various forms will have to be completed and it makes sense to prepare these prior to completion to save delays afterwards, particularly as you may well have one or two other matters to attend to, having just moved house.

Where you are buying with the aid of a mortgage, the lender's conveyancer will require you to send these forms to him or her so that he or she has them in time for completion. The conveyancer will then see to the post-completion work on your behalf.

The forms required for paying stamp duty land tax (SDLT 1) and registration (AP1) are explained further in Chapter 8, along with advice on how to complete them.

Lender's conveyancer's requirements

If you are buying with the aid of a mortgage and, as is likely, your lender's conveyancer intends to complete by post, make sure he or she has the following in good time (that is, at the latest the day before the date fixed for completion):

- the mortgage deed, executed (but not dated) by all the buyers
- forms AP1 and SDLT 1 (see above and Chapter 8)
- a cheque for the payment of any stamp duty land tax (made payable to the Inland Revenue*)
- a cheque for the payment of Land Registry fees (made payable to Land Registry)
- a cheque for the lender's conveyancer's fees (assuming he or she has asked for them on completion)
- results of the Land Registry search
- results of the bankruptcy search.

Completion

Completion is when you hand over the balance of the purchase price for the house and receive in return the deeds proving ownership – and the keys. Exactly what happens will depend upon whether you are completing through the post, and on whether or not you are financing the purchase with the aid of a mortgage.

Personal completion – no mortgage

If you are attending the completion you will still need to have arranged for the purchase money to be sent directly to the seller's conveyancer's bank account. This is a contractual requirement under the Standard Conditions. Expect to receive the following:

- the Transfer – check that it is the correct Transfer for the property you are buying, that it has been signed by all the sellers and that the signatures have been witnessed
- the Land Certificate – if the seller has a mortgage on the house there will be a Charge Certificate instead. As from 13 October 2003, Land and Charge certificates are no longer issued by Land Registry and those already issued no longer need to be handed over on completion – but they usually are as the seller has no further use for them. But it is of no concern if there is no Certificate handed over
- any guarantees or planning permissions referred to in the pre-contract enquiries – again, check they relate to the house you are buying
- if there is a mortgage on the property, you will eventually need Form DS1 or an END (proof that any existing mortgages have been paid off). It is unlikely that the seller will hand it over on completion, as he or she will need the purchase money in order to be able to pay off the loan, but you will need an undertaking from the conveyancer for the form to be sent to you when appropriate. The answers to your Completion Information Form will normally take effect as this undertaking, but if the seller's conveyancer stated that he or she would give you the undertaking only on completion, you should now make sure that you receive it. It should be in the form of a letter on the conveyancer's notepaper, addressed to you and stating that the conveyancer undertakes to pay off the existing mortgages on the property and to arrange for the END to be sent to Land Registry or to send you Form DS1 as soon as he or she receives it. Check that the undertaking promises to discharge all the mortgages revealed by the Official Copy Entries and your Form OS1 search – these will usually be expressly named in the undertaking

- receipt for chattels – if you have apportioned the sale price as a specific amount for chattels and a specific amount for the house in order to save stamp duty land tax, you will need a receipt for the amount you are paying for the chattels (the Transfer acts as a receipt for the money paid for the house). There is no need for this receipt to take any specific form, as long as it clearly acknowledges the receipt of the money and states that it is in relation to the chattels at the house you are buying

- pre-registration deeds – it is likely that the seller will also hand over to you a bundle of 'pre-registration deeds', and you will be asked to sign a 'schedule' or list of the deeds as a receipt for them. Before land is entered on the Land Register, ownership must be proven by production of title deeds, that is, documents showing the ownership of the land over a long period of years. Once the land is registered, these deeds no longer have such a purpose, but do not destroy them as they may be useful in the (rare) case of there being an error on the Register; they can also be of historical interest

- keys – it is perhaps more common for the keys to be handed over personally by the seller, or to be handed over by the estate agent, rather than by the conveyancer, on completion. If this is the case, you should ask the conveyancer for written authority authorising the seller or estate agent to hand over the keys, or ask the conveyancer, in your presence, to phone the seller or the estate agent to authorise the release of the keys. The conveyancer may be reluctant to do this, or could be distracted and forget to phone, resulting in the buyer having to hassle a seller or estate agent who has not been authorised to hand over the keys.

Completing by post

Completion by post may well seem a bit of an anticlimax if you have been doing the conveyancing yourself, as you will not be there to see the fruits of all your labour. However, it is more convenient for all concerned. Simply arrange for the money to be sent by your bank directly into the seller's conveyancer's account, and then send a letter explaining what you expect to be sent in return for the balance of the purchase price (that is, the documents mentioned above). Arrangements will also need to be made for handing over the keys.

Make sure you post the letter to the seller's conveyancer in ample time for completion. Do not leave things until the last minute and rely on next-day delivery of your letter, unless you are using some form of guaranteed delivery system. The seller should receive the letter the day before the date fixed for completion, so allow time for unexpected postal delays. Check also that the seller's conveyancer will check any matters that you would have checked had you attended personally.

As far as the keys are concerned, you will need to ask the seller's conveyancer to telephone the seller or the estate agent (depending upon who is going to hand you the keys) as soon as completion has taken place to authorise release of the keys to you. You should also ask the seller's conveyancer to phone you to let you know that completion has taken place, so that you will know when the keys should be available. Your letter should also inform the seller's conveyancer of the time of day when you expect the transfer of funds to take place.

Buying with the aid of a mortgage

When you are buying with the aid of a mortgage loan, it is likely that your lender's conveyancer will complete by post. If the conveyancer intends to complete by personal attendance, you will need to arrange a mutually convenient appointment with the seller's conveyancer so that you can both attend at the same time. Take the same steps as mentioned above, the only difference being that all the documentation will be handed over to your lender's conveyancer. All that you will be entitled to will be the keys and the receipt for the chattels.

If the lender's conveyancer is completing by post, it will be more convenient for you to do so as well. The keys will not be released to you until the seller's conveyancer has received both the money from yourself and the money from your lender. In both cases this will be sent directly to the seller's conveyancer's bank account. Again, all the documentation will be sent to your lender's conveyancer.

Dependent sales and purchases

Where you are selling your existing house and using the proceeds of the sale to buy your new house, the procedure to be followed will be basically the same but with one or two more complications.

It goes without saying that you will not be able to complete the purchase of the new house until you have sold the old one. It is also likely that there will be three sources of funds with which you are paying for the new house: the proceeds of the sale of the old house; the new mortgage loan; and possibly your own savings. You will need to arrange for the part of the purchase price you are providing personally to be sent to the seller's conveyancer's bank account in the usual way. The conveyancer acting for your existing lender will then arrange to send the balance of the proceeds of the sale of your existing house (after deducting the amount due to redeem the existing mortgage), together with the new mortgage loan, to the seller's conveyancer as before. Additional complications arise where there are different conveyancers acting for the lender on the house you are selling and the lender for the house you are buying. If this is the case, the conveyancer acting for the lender on the sale should be asked to send the net proceeds of the sale, after deducting the amount of the existing loan, to your seller's conveyancers and also to phone the conveyancer acting for your new lender to confirm that the old loan has been paid off. This conveyancer will then send the new loan to the seller's conveyancer in the usual way. It will be a term of the new loan that this will not be available to you unless and until the old loan is paid off – hence the need for this step.

Conclusion

It seems that there are a thousand and one things to do and remember when moving house, and if you are doing your own conveyancing the workload will be significantly increased. Bear this in mind when deciding whether or not to do your own conveyancing, particularly where a sale *and* purchase need to be completed on the same day. You will save yourself much work and worry on completion day if you choose to complete through the post rather than personally, and will therefore need to concentrate only on the practical aspects of moving. Either way, at the end of the day you should be the proud owner of a new home.

However, your job as conveyancer is not yet over; there is more work to be done as quickly as possible after completion if you are to avoid penalties and risk, and this is covered in the next chapter.

Chapter 8

Buying your house – post-completion matters

Although the word completion suggests that all the legal work is over, in fact there are still several important matters that you will need to deal with, in addition to all the usual problems that accompany moving into a new house.

If you have bought with the aid of a mortgage, the following will be carried out on your behalf by the lender's solicitor and you will be able to concentrate on settling into your new home. However, you should still read this chapter as the lender's solicitor will expect you to provide him or her with all the forms necessary to carry out this post-completion work. You should already have the draft forms ready to be handed over to the lender's solicitor prior to completion.

Receiving Form DS1

If there was an existing mortgage on the house, this will be paid off by the seller on completion. To prove that it is discharged the seller's lender will often execute Land Registry Form DS1. You (or your own lender's solicitor) will have received an undertaking from the seller's solicitor to forward this form as soon as possible after completion (expect to receive it within ten days or so). If you bought the house with the aid of a mortgage, this form will be sent to your lender's solicitor.

Form DS1 is set out in Appendix II. When you receive it make sure that all the boxes are completed correctly, that is, that the information in Boxes 1, 2, 4 and 5 is the same as that in the Official Copy Entries. Box 7 can be ignored and the form should be dated in Box 3 and executed by the lender in Box 8.

Stamping

The Transfer will need 'stamping' within 30 days of completion. This consists of two elements.

First, if the sale price was over £60,000 then stamp duty land tax, a government tax, is payable. Duty is based on the value of the property you are buying and is calculated on the whole of the purchase price (see Chapter 6 to find out how much you will have to pay); the cheque should be made payable to Inland Revenue.

In addition, whether or not any duty is payable, a Land Transaction Return giving details about the purchase and the buyer(s) must be given to the Inland Revenue by completing Form SDLT 1, again within 30 days of completion. This form is available only from the Inland Revenue. It should be completed in accordance with the guidance notes provided by the Inland Revenue – 40 pages of them!

You must comply with the 30-day time limit for stamping. Failure to do so will result in a financial penalty. Remember also that after you have dealt with the stamping, you then have to register the transaction at Land Registry, and there is a time limit for that too.

On receipt of a correctly completed SDLT 1 (and the correct amount of duty, where duty is payable), a certificate in Form SDLT 5 will be sent to you. This should then be sent to Land Registry with the application for registration.

Registration

After stamping has been effected and the Transfer returned by the Inland Revenue, you will need to apply to the appropriate Land Registry Office for registration as proprietor of the house. The application must be submitted within the protection period given by the pre-completion Form OS1 search. This protection ends 30 working days from the date the search was made, and this is clearly stated at the top of the result of the search. Complete Land Registry Form AP1 (see page 140) and send it to the Land Registry Office for the area in which the property is situated (see Appendix I) with the documents listed on the form and a cheque for the fee (see below); you should put the title number on the reverse of the cheque.

Completing Form AP1

Box 1 – insert the administrative area and postcode from the Official Copy Entries.

Box 2 – insert the title number from the Official Copy Entries.

Box 3 – this can be left blank.

Box 4 – place an X in the first box, against the 'whole of the title'.

Box 5 – list the applications as follows:

1. Discharge of registered charge (only insert this if the seller had a mortgage on the property). If the seller has more than one mortgage, then a separate entry should be made for each charge being discharged
2. Transfer
3. Charge (only insert this if you are buying with the aid of a mortgage).

In the column headed 'value' you must insert the price of the house, excluding chattels, alongside 'transfer' and the amount of the loan alongside 'charge'. Leave blank the column alongside any discharge of a Registered Charge.

There are no fees for discharging a Registered Charge or for registering the new charge, so the fee is assessed only on the value of the property transferred. To calculate the fee, see the Table on page 94 and then insert the amount being paid. You should then complete the payment method. This will be by cheque payable to Land Registry.

Box 6 – the documents lodged should be stated and numbered in the same order as the applications being made. So you should list first any and all Form DS1s relating to the discharge of existing mortgages. There should then follow the Transfer and any new mortgage. You will also need to include a photocopy of the new mortgage and this should be numbered as a separate document. Form SDLT 5 (proof of submission of Land Transaction Return) should also be included. Registration cannot be effected without this.

Box 7 – if you are buying with the aid of a mortgage, insert the lender's solicitor's address here. You can obtain this from the solicitor's notepaper. It is likely that the notepaper will refer to a 'DX number'; if so, you should include this rather than the postal address. The 'DX' (or Document Exchange) is a form of private mail system to which most solicitors belong. If there is no mortgage, you should insert your own address.

Box 8 – leave this box blank; the Title Information Document will then be sent to the address in Box 7.

Box 9 – this sets out the address of the new registered proprietor, that is, you. Insert an X in the first box, provided that the addresses on the Transfer are still the ones you wish to use; if not, you should complete the second box with details of the new address(es).

Box 10 – you are required to disclose to Land Registry any disclosable overriding interests that affect the land you are buying. See page 39 as to overriding interests. In effect, this means that you must disclose any easements (rights of way, drainage and so on) that affect the property but are not shown on the register. Often there will be none of these, in which case you can put an X in the first box. However, some such interests may be revealed by your inspection of the land or disclosed by the seller in the Property Information Form. If there are any such matters that come to your attention, you will need to place an X in the second box and then give brief details of the right on Form DI.

Box 11 – this can be left blank.

Do not sign or date the form; this will be attended to by the lender's solicitor if you are buying with the aid of a mortgage loan. If there is no mortgage, you should only sign and date the form when you are about to send it off to Land Registry.

The application must be received by the appropriate Land Registry Office no later than 9.30am on the day the protection period expires. Delivery after this date could mean that you will be bound by other entries which have been made on the Register since the date the search was made.

As the documentation being sent is proof of your ownership of the house, a guaranteed delivery postal or courier service should be used. And before sending the documents, you should take photocopies of them all – just in case!

Completing Form AP1

An example of Form AP1 can be found in Appendix II, and like all Land Registry forms it is simple to complete (see box above).

Receipt of the Title Information Document

Once Land Registry has processed your application, it will send you a Title Information Document relating to the house. This will contain up-to-date Official Copy Entries of the Register of your title and should show you as the owner of the house. Check this carefully to make sure it does not contain any unexpected entries. If you bought your house with the aid of a mortgage, the Title Information Document will be sent to the lender's solicitor.

Chapter 9

What to do if things go wrong – breach of contract

It is most unusual for a conveyancing transaction to go so far wrong that the parties end up in court suing each other. However, it is as well to be aware of your rights and responsibilities under the contract. It is not at all unusual for one or other of the parties to commit a minor breach of contract, for example by delaying completion, and again you need to be aware of your position should this happen.

The contract

Your rights and obligations are governed by the terms of the contract you have entered into. This chapter assumes that the contract incorporates the Standard Conditions of Sale, as this is most often the case. If the contract you have entered into does not incorporate the Standard Conditions, you will need to take professional advice.

The Standard Conditions of Sale (see Appendix II) deal with the most common examples of breach of contract and clearly set out what is to happen if a breach of contract arises, enabling matters to be resolved without the need to go to court.

Late completion

The most common problem is where one of the parties is unable to complete on the agreed completion date. There can be numerous reasons for late completion, for example the purchase money is late arriving (perhaps it was not requested from the lender in time), a removal van cannot be arranged for the fixed day, or there is a delay in signing the Transfer. Any delay in completion beyond the agreed date is a breach of contract entitling the innocent party to damages to compensate for the loss. However, the law does not allow the innocent party to treat the contract as terminated by the breach and thus refuse to proceed with it. He or she is required to give the other party time to sort out his or her affairs and complete, albeit a little late.

In many cases there is only a short delay in completion, and therefore no reason why matters cannot be resolved without the need for professional help.

Standard Condition 7.3 sets out the position with regard to delays. The party who is most at fault pays compensation to the other, the compensation being interest on the purchase price calculated at the rate specified in the contract (see page 54). The interest is payable for the period of the delay. The buyer pays interest only on the balance of the purchase price, that is, the agreed price less any deposit paid; if the seller is at fault, he or she pays interest on the full amount of the purchase price. For example, on a purchase of £100,000 where a £10,000 deposit has been paid and the buyer is three days late in completing, he or she will pay three days' interest at the contract rate on £90,000.

If as seller you feel that this sum does not adequately compensate you for the loss you have suffered, you may be entitled to additional damages for breach of contract, though this will almost inevitably lead to court proceedings. If you are seeking additional damages, or if the other party is attempting to claim additional damages from you, you should therefore seek professional advice. Note, however, that it is most unusual for either party to contemplate claiming additional damages in the case of a short delay.

As mentioned, Standard Condition 7.3 provides that the party who is most at fault pays compensation. However, it allows for the fact that the party unable to complete on time may not be the one who really caused the delay; the failure may be due to the knock-on effect of earlier delays incurred by the other party. For example, the seller may be unable to complete because he or she has not yet had time to sign the Transfer, and if this is because the buyer was late in sending the Transfer to the seller, then it is hardly fair to expect the seller to pay compensation.

To find out who is most at fault, you must refer to Standard Condition 4.3, which sets out a timetable for the various steps of the transaction. This can be used to see whether the buyer and seller have complied with the timetable and add up the various periods of default. The party whose default is the greatest is the one who will pay the compensation, and this compensation is payable for the period that the party's default is greater than that of the other. However, if the actual delay in completion is shorter than this, interest is only payable for the period of actual delay.

This principle of relative fault is horrendously complicated. It is therefore often ignored in practice and a simplistic view adopted, for example the buyer was three days late in completing, therefore he or she pays three days' interest. Example 1 shows how the Standard Condition should be applied.

EXAMPLE 1

Under Standard Condition 4.3, a seller is three days late in delivering his evidence of title. His buyer is then five days late in delivering her requisitions and a further four days late in sending the draft Transfer. Completion then takes place two days late because the seller is not yet ready to complete.

To assess who is liable to pay compensation, it is necessary to add up each party's total period of default. Here the seller's total default adds up to five days, and the buyer's to nine days. The buyer's default thus exceeds the seller's by four days and so the buyer will pay compensation. Although the buyer's default exceeded the seller's by four days, the actual delay in completion was only two days, and she will therefore pay only two days' interest.

There are further complications to bear in mind; the timetable laid down by Standard Condition 4.3 refers to 'working days', that is, excluding weekends and public holidays. However, in calculating the actual delay in completion, every day must be included, and not just working days. So, pre-completion, doing something on a Monday when it should have been completed on a Friday will count as one working day's delay; a similar delay in completion from Friday to Monday will count as three days' delay. This timetable is also based on a lengthy gap between exchange and completion; if, as is now usual, there is only a short gap between exchange and completion, that is, less than 15 working days, then the timetable laid down by Standard Condition 4.3 has to be reduced proportionately (see Standard Condition 4.3.4). It is therefore little wonder that this principle is often ignored.

When completion is deemed late

Under Standard Condition 6.1.2, if completion has not taken place by 2pm on a particular day, then completion is deemed to take place on the next working day, even if it actually takes place at, say, 4pm the same day. This is because of the difficulty of gaining access to funds outside normal banking hours; the 2pm deadline gives ample time for the money to be paid into an account and withdrawn, if necessary.

This deemed delay is only relevant in relation to the compensation provisions. So, if completion was fixed for Friday and did not take place until 3pm that day, it would be deemed to take place on the following Monday (assuming that the Monday was not a public holiday), and so the buyer would have to pay three days' interest. However, if the parties had expressly agreed that completion was not to take place until 3pm, then this provision would not apply. Equally, the Standard Conditions state that if the seller has not vacated the house by 2pm then there is no need to pay the day's interest if completion does not take place until after that time.

Protracted delays/refusal to complete

It is unlikely that there will be any protracted delays in completion or that one party or the other will simply refuse to complete. However, the following situations can arise.

• **You don't want to complete** Once you have entered into the contract you are legally bound to go through with the sale or purchase. It is only in exceptional circumstances that you can withdraw at this stage. If you wish to do so, seek professional advice straight away; you may be able to withdraw from the contract or claim compensation if the seller has deliberately omitted to disclose details of an incumbrance on the property or if he or she has made a misrepresentation to you. A misrepresentation is a statement of fact which you took into account when you decided to buy the property and which you subsequently discover to be untrue. Standard Condition 7.1 sets out your rights in such cases.

- **The other party refuses to complete** Again, it will only be in exceptional circumstances that he or she has such a right, but in the event of this you should seek professional advice immediately.
- **There is a long delay after the agreed completion date and completion has still not taken place** It may be you who is unable to complete, or the other party. Either way, it is unreasonable to expect the other party to wait forever.

The deposit

If the buyer refuses to complete without good cause, the seller is entitled to keep the deposit paid, even if his or her loss is less than this. A buyer must therefore think very carefully before refusing to complete. Irrespective of his or her liability to pay damages for breach of contract, he or she will lose the deposit already paid.

If the buyer does have good grounds to refuse to proceed, he or she will be entitled to the return of his or her deposit. However, in reality, if the seller does not accept that the buyer has good grounds, the only way the buyer can actually get back the deposit may be by commencing court proceedings, which can be expensive and slow.

Damages for breach of contract

Damages are payable when either party to a contract is in breach of that contract. The damages are assessed by the court to compensate the innocent party for the loss suffered by the other party's breach of contract. The idea is to maintain the position that the innocent party would have been in had the contract been properly performed. Therefore, if as a result of one party's refusal to complete, the other party has to move into temporary accommodation, or a buyer has to buy another property at a higher price, the cost of these will be recoverable. Note also that if you are in a chain transaction, a breach of contract by one party to one contract may have a knock-on effect with regard to the other transactions in the chain. So, if you refuse to buy from your seller and as a result are in breach of contract, this will probably mean that your seller will not be able to proceed with the purchase of his or her new house, as the money to buy it will not be available. That will put him or her in breach of that contract and liable to pay damages as a result. Your seller will then have a claim for damages against you because of your breach and will be entitled to include in that claim the damages he or she has to pay out in relation to his or her own purchase.

Notice to complete

Standard Condition 6.8 allows the innocent party to serve a 'notice to complete'. This is a notice served on the delaying party requiring him or her to complete within ten working days. If this notice is not complied with, the party who is ready to complete can then treat the contract as terminated. A seller can then start looking for another buyer, keeping the deposit, or a buyer can then claim back his or her deposit and look for somewhere else to buy. There would also be a claim for damages for breach of contract.

If the completion date has passed and you are not certain of being able to complete within a few days after the agreed date, you run the risk of not being able to comply with a notice to complete and you should seek professional advice immediately. Some solicitors will serve a notice to complete as soon as the agreed date for completion has passed in order to protect their client's position. Just because the notice to complete has expired does not mean that the innocent party is forced to treat the contract as discharged; he or she can still give the delaying party another chance to sort things out and complete. However, if the notice is served immediately it does give the innocent party a wider choice of options if there is not a speedy completion.

If you receive a notice to complete and you are not certain that you can complete within the ten working days specified, you must again seek professional advice.

If the other party delays for more than a few days after the agreed date, you should also seek professional advice, and you must not serve a notice to complete until you have obtained advice. Various pre-conditions need to be satisfied before you can serve such a notice, and you must comply with them. Once served, a notice to complete is binding upon both parties. You do not want to serve a notice and then find that *you* are the one unable to complete, as the other party would then have the right to terminate the contract against you.

Death

An exceptional cause of a delay in completion is the death of one or other of the parties.

The problems this will cause to the conveyancing transaction are probably the last thing the family of the deceased will be concerned with, but will obviously be of great concern to the other party to the transaction.

The law is quite clear on this matter. On the death of a party to a contract, the contract continues to be enforceable. If a will has been left, then an executor may have been appointed to deal with the deceased's affairs. If there is no appointed executor, a member of the deceased's family will be entitled to take on the role of administrator of the deceased's property. Either way, the contract will be enforceable against the administrator or executor.

On the death of the seller, it is likely that the transaction will still proceed. It is inevitable, however, that there will be a delay. This is so whether a sole seller dies or where one of two co-sellers dies. The deceased's relatives will have to arrange a funeral, and perhaps arrange for the house to be cleared. Legal formalities may be necessary before the sale can proceed. The executor or administrator will need to be formally appointed by the court before the sale can proceed.

On the death of a buyer, it is unlikely that the transaction can proceed. If the deceased was buying with the aid of a mortgage loan, the lender will no longer proceed with the loan. On the death of one of two joint purchasers, it may be that the lender will still withdraw the loan if the income of the survivor is insufficient to support the repayments. In such a case, the seller will be entitled to keep the deposit and to claim any further loss suffered as damages for breach of contract.

In the unlikely event that a party to a conveyancing contract dies, it will be necessary to seek professional advice as to how you might be affected.

Areas served by and addresses of District Land Registries

Administrative Area	Land Registry Office
Bath & North East Somerset	Plymouth
Bedfordshire	Peterborough
Blackburn with Darwen	Lancashire
Bournemouth	Weymouth
Bracknell Forest	Gloucester
Brighton & Hove	Portsmouth
Bristol	Gloucester
Buckinghamshire	Leicester
Cambridgeshire	Peterborough
Cheshire	Birkenhead (Rosebrae)
Cornwall	Plymouth
Cumbria	Durham (Boldon House)
Darlington	Durham (Southfield House)
Derby (City)	Nottingham (West)
Derbyshire	Nottingham (West)
Devon	Plymouth
Dorset	Weymouth
Durham	Durham (Southfield House)
East Riding of Yorkshire	York
East Sussex	Portsmouth
Essex	Peterborough
Gloucestershire	Gloucester
Greater Manchester	Lytham

Administrative Area	Land Registry Office
Halton	Birkenhead (Rosebrae)
Hampshire	Weymouth
Hartlepool	Durham (Southfield House)
Herefordshire	Telford
Hertfordshire	Stevenage
Isle of Wight	Portsmouth
Isles of Scilly	Plymouth
Kent	Tunbridge Wells
Kingston upon Hull	Kingston upon Hull
Lancashire	Lancashire
Leicester	Leicester
Leicestershire	Leicester
Lincolnshire	Kingston upon Hull
Luton	Peterborough
Medway	Tunbridge Wells
Merseyside	Birkenhead (Old Market)
Middlesbrough	Durham (Southfield House)
Milton Keynes	Leicester
Norfolk	Kingston upon Hull
North East Lincolnshire	Kingston upon Hull
North Lincolnshire	Kingston upon Hull
North Somerset	Plymouth
North Yorkshire	York
Northamptonshire	Leicester
Northumberland	Durham (Southfield House)
Nottingham	Nottingham (East)
Nottinghamshire	Nottingham (East)
Oxfordshire	Gloucester
Peterborough	Peterborough
Plymouth	Plymouth
Poole	Weymouth
Portsmouth	Portsmouth
Reading	Gloucester
Redcar & Cleveland	Durham (Southfield House)
Rutland	Leicester
Shropshire	Telford

Administrative Area	Land Registry Office
Slough	Gloucester
Somerset (Mendip/ South Somerset)	Weymouth
Somerset (remainder)	Plymouth
South Gloucestershire	Gloucester
South Yorkshire	Nottingham (West)
Southampton	Weymouth
Southend on Sea	Peterborough
Staffordshire	Birkenhead (Old Market)
Stockton on Tees	Durham (Southfield House)
Stoke on Trent	Birkenhead (Old Market)
Suffolk	Kingston upon Hull
Surrey	Durham (Boldon House)
Swindon	Weymouth
Thurrock	Peterborough
Torbay	Plymouth
Tyne & Wear	Durham (Southfield House)
Warrington	Birkenhead (Rosebrae)
Warwickshire	Gloucester
West Berkshire	Gloucester
West Midlands	Coventry
West Sussex	Portsmouth
West Yorkshire	Nottingham (West)
Wiltshire	Weymouth
Windsor & Maidenhead	Gloucester
Wokingham	Gloucester
Worcestershire	Coventry
Wrekin	Telford
York	York

Wales/Cymru

All areas	Land Registry – Wales Office

Greater London

Barking & Dagenham	Stevenage
Barnet	Swansea
Bexley	Croydon

Administrative Area	Land Registry Office
Brent	Harrow
Bromley	Croydon
Camden	Harrow
City of London	Harrow
City of Westminster	Harrow
Croydon	Croydon
Ealing	Swansea
Enfield	Swansea
Greenwich	Telford
Hackney	Stevenage
Hammersmith & Fulham	Birkenhead (Rosebrae)
Haringey	Swansea
Harrow	Harrow
Havering	Stevenage
Hillingdon	Swansea
Hounslow	Swansea
Inner & Middle Temples	Harrow
Islington	Harrow
Kensington & Chelsea	Birkenhead (Rosebrae)
Kingston upon Thames	Croydon
Lambeth	Telford
Lewisham	Telford
Merton	Croydon
Newham	Stevenage
Redbridge	Stevenage
Richmond upon Thames	Telford
Southwark	Telford
Sutton	Croydon
Tower Hamlets	Stevenage
Waltham Forest	Stevenage
Wandsworth	Telford

Addresses of Land Registry Offices

Website address *www.landreg.gov.uk*

Birkenhead (Old Market)
Old Market House
Hamilton Street
Birkenhead
Merseyside CH41 5FL
Tel: 0151-473 1110
Fax: 0151-473 0251

Birkenhead (Rosebrae)
Rosebrae Court
Woodside Ferry Approach
Birkenhead
Merseyside CH41 6DU
Tel: 0151-472 6666
Fax: 0151-472 6789

Coventry
Leigh Court
Torrington Avenue
Tile Hill
Coventry CV4 9XZ
Tel: 024-7686 0860
Fax: 024-7686 0021

Croydon
Sunley House
Bedford Park
Croydon CR9 3LE
Tel: 020-8781 9103
Fax: 020-8781 9110

Durham (Boldon House)
Boldon House
Wheatlands Way
Pity Me
Durham DH1 5GJ
Tel: 0191-301 2345
Fax: 0191-301 2300

Durham (Southfield House)
Southfield House
Southfield Way
Durham DH1 5TR
Tel: 0191-301 3500
Fax: 0191-301 0020

Gloucester
Twyver House
Bruton Way
Gloucester GL1 1DQ
Tel: (01452) 511111
Fax: (01452) 510050

Harrow
Lyon House
Lyon Road
Harrow
Middlesex HA1 2EU
Tel: 020-8235 1181
Fax: 020-8862 0176

Kingston upon Hull
Earle House
Colonial Street
Hull HU2 8JN
Tel: (01482) 223244
Fax: (01482) 224278

Lancashire
Wrea Brook Court
Lytham Road
Warton PR4 1TE
Tel: (01772) 836700
Fax: (01772) 836970

Leicester
Westbridge Place
Leicester LE3 5DR
Tel: 0116-265 4000
Fax: 0116-265 4008

Lytham
Birkenhead House
East Beach
Lytham St. Annes
Lancashire FY8 5AB
Tel: (01253) 849849
Fax: (01253) 840001

Nottingham (East)
Robins Wood Road
Nottingham NG8 3RQ
Tel: 0115-906 5353
Fax: 0115-936 0036

Nottingham (West)
Chalfont Drive
Nottingham NG8 3RN
Tel: 0115-935 1166
Fax: 0115-935 0038

Peterborough
Touthill Close
City Road
Peterborough PE1 1XN
Tel: (01733) 288288
Fax: (01733) 280022

Plymouth
Plumer House
Tailyour Road
Crownhill
Plymouth PL6 5HY
Tel: (01752) 636000
Fax: (01752) 636161

Portsmouth
St Andrew's Court
St Michael's Road
Portsmouth
Hampshire PO1 2JH
Tel: 023-9276 8888
Fax: 023-9276 8768

Stevenage
Brickdale House
Swingate
Stevenage
Herts SG1 1XG
Tel: (01438) 788889
Fax: (01438) 785460

Swansea (Titles in England)
Ty Bryn Glas
High Street
Swansea SA1 1PW
Tel: (01792) 458877
Fax: (01792) 473236

Telford
Parkside Court
Hall Park Way
Telford TF3 4LR
Tel: (01952) 290355
Fax: (01952) 290356

Tunbridge Wells
Forest Court
Forest Road
Tunbridge Wells
Kent TN2 5AQ
Tel: (01892) 510015
Fax: (01892) 510032

Weymouth
Melcombe Court
1 Cumberland Drive
Weymouth
Dorset DT4 9TT
Tel: (01305) 363636
Fax: (01305) 363646

York
James House
James Street
York YO10 3YZ
Tel: (01904) 450000
Fax: (01904) 450086

Wales/Cymru
(Titles in Wales)
Ty Cwm Tawe
Phoenix Way
Llansamlet
Swansea SA7 9FQ
Tel: (01792) 355000
Fax: (01792) 355055

Land Charges Department
Plumer House
Tailyour Road
Crownhill
Plymouth PL6 5HY
Tel: (01752) 636666
Fax: (01752) 636699

Land Registry Head Office
32 Lincoln's Inn Fields
London WC2A 3PH
Tel: 020-7917 8888
Fax: 020-7955 0110

Specimen forms

LAND REGISTRY

TITLE NUMBER: NS 975321
Edition date: 1 May 1985

A: Property Register

This register describes the land and estate comprised in the title.

COUNTY	DISTRICT
HUMBERSIDE	WESTFORD

1. (19 February 1960) The freehold land shown and edged with red on the plan of the above title filed at the Registry and being 10, Manor Drive, Westford, Humbershire HS11 2AB.

B: Proprietorship Register

This register specifies the class of title and identifies the owner. It contains any entries that affect the right of disposal.

Title Absolute

1. (1 May 1985) Proprietor(s): ROGER EVANS of 10, Manor Drive, Westford, Humbershire HS11 2AB.

C: Charges Register

This register contains any charges and other matters that affect the land.

1. (19 February 1960) A Conveyance of the land in this title dated 9 August 1952 made between (1) Sir James Fawcett (Vendor) and (2) Harold Hawtree (Purchaser) contains the following covenants:

    'The Purchaser with the intent and so as to bind the property hereby conveyed and to benefit and protect the retained land of the Vendor lying to the south of the land hereby conveyed hereby covenants with the Vendor that he and his successors in title will at all times observe and perform the stipulations and conditions set out in the schedule hereto.'

    THE SCHEDULE ABOVE REFERRED TO

    'Not to build or allow to be built on the property any building without the written consent of the Vendor or his successors in title.'

2. (1 May 1985) REGISTERED CHARGE dated 19 April 1985 to secure the moneys including the further advances therein mentioned.

3. (1 May 1985) Proprietor(s): HUMBERSHIRE AND COUNTIES BANK PLC of County House, Westford, Humbershire HS11 8YU.

END OF REGISTER

NOTE: A date at the beginning of an entry is the date on which the entry was made in the Register.

NOTE: THE TITLE PLAN HAS NOT BEEN REPRODUCED.

SPECIMEN

STANDARD CONDITIONS OF SALE (FOURTH EDITION)
(NATIONAL CONDITIONS OF SALE 24TH EDITION,
LAW SOCIETY'S CONDITIONS OF SALE 2003)

1. GENERAL

1.1 Definitions

1.1.1 In these conditions:
- (a) 'accrued interest' means:
  - (i) if money has been placed on deposit or in a building society share account, the interest actually earned
  - (ii) otherwise, the interest which might reasonably have been earned by depositing the money at interest on seven days' notice of withdrawal with a clearing bank less, in either case, any proper charges for handling the money
- (b) 'chattels price' means any separate amount payable for chattels included in the contract
- (c) 'clearing bank' means a bank which is a shareholder in CHAPS Clearing Co. Limited
- (d) 'completion date' has the meaning given in condition 6.1.1
- (e) 'contract rate' means the Law Society's interest rate from time to time in force
- (f) 'conveyancer' means a solicitor, barrister, duly certified notary public, licensed conveyancer or recognised body under sections 9 or 23 of the Administration of Justice Act 1985
- (g) 'direct credit' means a direct transfer of cleared funds to an account nominated by the seller's conveyancer and maintained by a clearing bank
- (h) 'lease' includes sub-lease, tenancy and agreement for a lease or sub-lease
- (i) 'notice to complete' means a notice requiring completion of the contract in accordance with condition 6
- (j) 'public requirement' means any notice, order or proposal given or made (whether before or after the date of the contract) by a body acting on statutory authority
- (k) 'requisition' includes objection
- (l) 'transfer' includes conveyance and assignment
- (m) 'working day' means any day from Monday to Friday (inclusive) which is not Christmas Day, Good Friday or a statutory Bank Holiday.

1.1.2 In these conditions the terms 'absolute title' and 'official copies' have the special meanings given to them by the Land Registration Act 2002.

1.1.3 A party is ready, able and willing to complete:
- (a) if he could be, but for the default of the other party, and
- (b) in the case of the seller, even though the property remains subject to a mortgage, if the amount to be paid on completion

enables the property to be transferred freed of all mortgages (except any to which the sale is expressly subject).

1.1.4 These conditions apply except as varied or excluded by the contract.

1.2 Joint parties

If there is more than one seller or more than one buyer, the obligations which they undertake can be enforced against them all jointly or against each individually.

1.3 Notices and documents

1.3.1 A notice required or authorised by the contract must be in writing.

1.3.2 Giving a notice or delivering a document to a party's conveyancer has the same effect as giving or delivering it to that party.

1.3.3 Where delivery of the original document is not essential, a notice or document is validly given or sent if it is sent:

(a) by fax, or

(b) by e-mail to an e-mail address for the intended recipient given in the contract.

1.3.4 Subject to conditions 1.3.5 to 1.3.7, a notice is given and a document is delivered when it is received.

1.3.5 (a) A notice or document sent through a document exchange is received when it is available for collection

(b) A notice or document which is received after 4.00pm on a working day, or on a day which is not a working day, is to be treated as having been received on the next working day

(c) An automated response to a notice or document sent by e-mail that the intended recipient is out of the office is to be treated as proof that the notice or document was not received.

1.3.6 Condition 1.3.7 applies unless there is proof:

(a) that a notice or document has not been received, or

(b) of when it was received.

1.3.7 A notice or document sent by the following means is treated as having been received as follows:

(a)	by first-class post:	before 4.00pm on the second working day after posting
(b)	by second-class post:	before 4.00pm on the third working day after posting
(c)	through a document exchange:	before 4.00pm on the first working day after the day on which it would normally be available for collection by the addressee
(d)	by fax:	one hour after despatch
(e)	by e-mail:	before 4.00pm on the first working day after despatch.

1.4 VAT

1.4.1 An obligation to pay money includes an obligation to pay any value added tax chargeable in respect of that payment.

1.4.2 All sums made payable by the contract are exclusive of value added tax.

1.5 Assignment

The buyer is not entitled to transfer the benefit of the contract.

2. FORMATION

2.1 Date

2.1.1 If the parties intend to make a contract by exchanging duplicate copies by post or through a document exchange, the contract is made when the last copy is posted or deposited at the document exchange.

2.1.2 If the parties' conveyancers agree to treat exchange as taking place before duplicate copies are actually exchanged, the contract is made as so agreed.

2.2 Deposit

2.2.1 The buyer is to pay or send a deposit of 10 per cent of the total of the purchase price and the chattels price no later then the date of the contract.

2.2.2 If a cheque tendered in payment of all or part of the deposit is dishonoured when first presented, the seller may, within seven working days of being notified that the cheque has been dishonoured, give notice to the buyer that the contract is discharged by the buyer's breach.

2.2.3 Conditions 2.2.4 to 2.2.6 do not apply on a sale by auction.

2.2.4 The deposit is to be paid by direct credit or to the seller's conveyancer by a cheque drawn on a solicitor's or licensed conveyancer's client account.

2.2.5 If before completion date the seller agrees to buy another property in England and Wales for his residence, he may use all or any part of the deposit as a deposit in that transaction to be held on terms to the same effect as this condition and condition 2.2.6.

2.2.6 Any deposit or part of a deposit not being used in accordance with condition 2.2.5 is to be held by the seller's conveyancer as stakeholder on terms that on completion it is paid to the seller with accrued interest.

2.3 Auctions

2.3.1 On a sale by auction the following conditions apply to the property and, if it is sold in lots, to each lot.

2.3.2 The sale is subject to a reserve price.

2.3.3 The seller, or a person on his behalf, may bid up to the reserve price.

2.3.4 The auctioneer may refuse any bid.

2.3.5 If there is a dispute about a bid, the auctioneer may resolve the dispute or restart the auction at the last undisputed bid.

2.3.6 The deposit is to be paid to the auctioneer as agent for the seller.

3. MATTERS AFFECTING THE PROPERTY

3.1 Freedom from incumbrances

3.1.1 The seller is selling the property free from incumbrances, other than those mentioned in condition 3.1.2.

3.1.2 The incumbrances subject to which the property is sold are:

    (a) those specified in the contract

    (b) those discoverable by inspection of the property before the contract

    (c) those the seller does not and could not reasonably know about

    (d) entries made before the date of the contract in any public register, except those maintained by HM Land Registry or its Land Charges Department or by Companies House

    (e) public requirements.

3.1.3 After the contract is made, the seller is to give the buyer written details without delay of any new public requirement and of anything in writing which he learns about concerning a matter covered by condition 3.1.2.

3.1.4 The buyer is to bear the cost of complying with any outstanding public requirement and is to indemnify the seller against any liability resulting from a public requirement.

3.2 Physical state

3.2.1 The buyer accepts the property in the physical state it is in at the date of the contract unless the seller is building or converting it.

3.2.2 A leasehold property is sold subject to any subsisting breach of a condition or tenant's obligation relating to the physical state of the property which renders the lease liable to forfeiture.

3.2.3 A sub-lease is granted subject to any subsisting breach of a condition or tenant's obligation relating to the physical state of the property which renders the seller's own lease liable to forfeiture.

3.3 Leases affecting the property

3.3.1 The following provisions apply if any part of the property is sold subject to a lease.

3.3.2 (a) The seller having provided the buyer with full details of each lease or copies of the documents embodying the lease terms, the buyer is treated as entering into the contract knowing and fully accepting those terms.

    (b) The seller is to inform the buyer without delay if the lease ends or if the seller learns of any application by the tenant in connection with the lease; the seller is then to act as the buyer reasonably directs, and the buyer is to indemnify him against all consequent loss and expense.

(c)   Except with the buyer's consent, the seller is not to agree to any proposal to change the lease terms nor to take any step to end the lease.

(d)   The seller is to inform the buyer without delay of any change to the lease terms which may be proposed or agreed.

(e)   The buyer is to indemnify the seller against all claims arising from the lease after actual completion; this includes claims which are unenforceable against a buyer for want of registration.

(f)   The seller takes no responsibility for what rent is lawfully recoverable, nor for whether or how any legislation affects the lease.

(g)   If the let land is not wholly within the property, the seller may apportion the rent.

3.4 Retained land

Where after the transfer the seller will be retaining land near the property:

(a)   the buyer will have no right of light or air over the retained land, but

(b)   in other respects the seller and the buyer will each have the rights over the land of the other which they would have had if they were two separate buyers to whom the seller had made simultaneous transfers of the property and the retained land. The transfer is to contain appropriate express terms.

4. TITLE AND TRANSFER

4.1 Proof of title

4.1.1 Without cost to the buyer, the seller is to provide the buyer with proof of the title to the property and of his ability to transfer it, or to procure its transfer.

4.1.2 Where the property has a registered title the proof is to include official copies of the items referred to in rules 134(1)(a) and (b) and 135(1)(a) of the Land Registration Rules 2003, so far as they are not to be discharged or overridden at or before completion.

4.1.3 Where the property has an unregistered title, the proof is to include:

(a)   an abstract of title or an epitome of title with photocopies of the documents, and

(b)   production of every document or an abstract, epitome or copy of it with an original marking by a conveyancer either against the original or an examined abstract or an examined copy.

4.2 Requisitions

4.2.1 The buyer may not raise requisitions:

(a)   on the title shown by the seller taking the steps described in condition 4.1.1, before the contract was made

(b)   in relation to the matters covered by condition 3.1.2.

4.2.2 Notwithstanding condition 4.2.1, the buyer may, within six working days of a matter coming to his attention after the contract was made, raise written requisitions on that matter. In that event, steps 3 and 4 in condition 4.3.1 apply.

4.2.3 On the expiry of the relevant time limit under condition 4.2.2 or condition 4.3.1, the buyer loses his right to raise requisitions or to make observations.

4.3 Timetable

4.3.1 Subject to condition 4.2 and to the extent that the seller did not take the steps described in condition 4.1.1 before the contract was made, the following are the steps for deducing and investigating the title to the property to be taken within the following time limits:

Step	Time Limit
1. The seller is to comply with condition 4.1.1	Immediately after making the contract
2. The buyer may raise written requisitions	Six working days after either the date of the contract or the date of delivery of the seller's proof of title on which the requisitions are raised, whichever is the later
3. The seller is to reply in writing to any requisitions raised	Four working days after receiving the requisitions
4. The buyer may make written observations on the seller's replies	Three working days after receiving the replies

The time limit on the buyer's right to raise requisitions applies even where the seller supplies incomplete evidence of his title, but the buyer may, within six working days from delivery of any further evidence, raise further requisitions resulting from that evidence.

4.3.2 The parties are to take the following steps to prepare and agree the transfer of the property within the following time limits:

Step	Time Limit
A. The buyer is to send the seller a draft transfer	At least twelve working days before completion date
B. The seller is to approve or revise that draft and either return it or retain it for use as the actual transfer	Four working days after delivery of the draft
C. If the draft is returned the buyer is to send an engrossment to the seller	At least five working days before completion date

4.3.3 Periods of time under conditions 4.3.1 and 4.3.2 may run concurrently.

4.3.4 If the period between the date of the contract and completion date is less than 15 working days, the time limits in conditions 4.2.2, 4.3.1 and 4.3.2 are to be reduced by the same proportion as that period bears to the period of 15 working days. Fractions of a working day are to be rounded down except that the time limit to perform any step is not to be less than one working day.

4.4 Defining the property

4.4.1 The seller need not:

(a)   prove the exact boundaries of the property

(b)   prove who owns fences, ditches, hedges or walls

(c)   separately identify parts of the property with different titles further than he may be able to do from information in his possession.

4.4.2 The buyer may, if it is reasonable, require the seller to make or obtain, pay for and hand over a statutory declaration about facts relevant to the matters mentioned in condition 4.4.1. The form of the declaration is to be agreed by the buyer, who must not unreasonably withhold his agreement.

4.5 Rents and rentcharges

The fact that a rent or rentcharge, whether payable or receivable by the owner of the property, has been, or will on completion be, informally apportioned is not to be regarded as a defect in title.

4.6 Transfer

4.6.1 The buyer does not prejudice his right to raise requisitions, or to require replies to any raised, by taking any steps in relation to preparing or agreeing the transfer.

4.6.2 Subject to condition 4.6.3, the seller is to transfer the property with full title guarantee.

4.6.3 The transfer is to have effect as if the disposition is expressly made subject to all matters covered by condition 3.1.2.

4.6.4 If after completion the seller will remain bound by any obligation affecting the property which was disclosed to the buyer before the contract was made, but the law does not imply any covenant by the buyer to indemnify the seller against liability for future breaches of it:

(a)   the buyer is to covenant in the transfer to indemnify the seller against liability for any future breach of the obligation and to perform it from then on, and

(b)   if required by the seller, the buyer is to execute and deliver to the seller on completion a duplicate transfer prepared by the buyer.

4.6.5 The seller is to arrange at his expense that, in relation to every document of title which the buyer does not receive on completion, the buyer is to have the benefit of:

(a)   a written acknowledgement of his right to its production, and

(b)   a written undertaking for its safe custody (except while it is held by a mortgagee or by someone in a fiduciary capacity).

5. PENDING COMPLETION

5.1 Responsibility for property

5.1.1 The seller will transfer the property in the same physical state as it was at the date of the contract (except for fair wear and tear), which means that the seller retains the risk until completion.

5.1.2 If at any time before completion the physical state of the property makes it unusable for its purpose at the date of the contract:

(a)   the buyer may rescind the contract

(b)   the seller may rescind the contract where the property has become unusable for that purpose as a result of damage against which the seller could not reasonably have insured, or which it is not legally possible for the seller to make good.

5.1.3 The seller is under no obligation to the buyer to insure the property.

5.1.4 Section 47 of the Law of Property Act 1925 does not apply.

5.2 Occupation by buyer

5.2.1 If the buyer is not already lawfully in the property, and the seller agrees to let him into occupation, the buyer occupies on the following terms.

5.2.2 The buyer is a licensee and not a tenant. The terms of the licence are that the buyer:

(a)   cannot transfer it

(b)   may permit members of his household to occupy the property

(c)   is to pay or indemnify the seller against all outgoings and other expenses in respect of the property

(d)   is to pay the seller a fee calculated at the contract rate on a sum equal to the purchase price and the chattels price (less any deposit paid) for the period of the licence

(e)   is entitled to any rents and profits from any part of the property which he does not occupy

(f)   is to keep the property in as good a state of repair as it was in when he went into occupation (except for fair wear and tear) and is not to alter it

(g)   is to insure the property in a sum which is not less than the purchase price against all risks in respect of which comparable premises are normally insured

(h)   is to quit the property when the licence ends.

5.2.3 On the creation of the buyer's licence, condition 5.1 ceases to apply, which means that the buyer then assumes the risk until completion.

5.2.4 The buyer is not in occupation for the purposes of this condition if he merely exercises rights of access given solely to do work agreed by the seller.

5.2.5 The buyer's licence ends on the earliest of: completion date, rescission of the contract or when five working days' notice given by one party to the other takes effect.

5.2.6 If the buyer is in occupation of the property after his licence has come to an end and the contract is subsequently completed he is to pay the seller compensation for his continued occupation calculated at the same rate as the fee mentioned in condition 5.2.2(d).

5.2.7 The buyer's right to raise requisitions is unaffected.

6. COMPLETION

6.1 Date

6.1.1 Completion date is twenty working days after the date of the contract but time is not of the essence of the contract unless a notice to complete has been served.

6.1.2 If the money due on completion is received after 2.00pm, completion is to be treated, for the purposes only of conditions 6.3 and 7.3, as taking place on the next working day as a result of the buyer's default.

6.1.3 Condition 6.1.2 does not apply and the seller is treated as in default if:

(i)   the sale is with vacant possession of the property or any part of it, and

(ii) the buyer is ready, able and willing to complete but does not pay the money due on completion until after 2.00pm because the seller has not vacated the property or that part by that time

6.2 Arrangements and place

6.2.1 The buyer's conveyancer and the seller's conveyancer are to co-operate in agreeing arrangements for completing the contract.

6.2.2 Completion is to take place in England and Wales, either at the seller's conveyancer's office or at some other place which the seller reasonably specifies.

6.3 Apportionments

6.3.1 Income and outgoings of the property are to be apportioned between the parties so far as the change of ownership on completion will affect entitlement to receive or liability to pay them.

6.3.2 If the whole property is sold with vacant possession or the seller exercises his option in condition 7.3.4, apportionment is to be made with effect from the date of actual completion; otherwise, it is to be made from completion date.

6.3.3 In apportioning any sum, it is to be assumed that the seller owns the property until the end of the day from which apportionment is made and that the sum accrues from day to day at the rate at which it is payable on that day.

6.3.4 For the purpose of apportioning income and outgoings, it is to be assumed that they accrue at an equal daily rate throughout the year.

6.3.5 When a sum to be apportioned is not known or easily ascertainable at completion, a provisional apportionment is to be made according to the best estimate available. As soon as the amount is known, a final apportionment is to be made and notified to the other party. Any resulting balance is to be paid no more than ten working days later, and if not then paid the balance is to bear interest at the contract rate from then until payment.

6.3.6 Compensation payable under condition 5.2.6 is not to be apportioned.

6.4 Amount payable

The amount payable by the buyer on completion is the purchase price and the chattels price (less any deposit already paid to the seller or his agent) adjusted to take account of:

(a) apportionments made under condition 6.3

(b) any compensation to be paid or allowed under condition 7.3.

6.5 Title deeds

6.5.1 As soon as the buyer has complied with all his obligations on completion the seller must hand over the documents of title.

6.5.2 Condition 6.5.1 does not apply to any documents of title relating to land being retained by the seller after completion.

6.6 Rent receipts

The buyer is to assume that whoever gave any receipt for a payment of rent or service charge which the seller produces was the person or the agent of the person then entitled to that rent or service charge.

6.7 Means of payment

The buyer is to pay the money due on completion by direct credit and, if appropriate, an unconditional release of a deposit held by a stakeholder.

6.8 Notice to complete

6.8.1 At any time on or after completion date, a party who is ready, able and willing to complete may give the other a notice to complete.

6.8.2 The parties are to complete the contract within ten working days of giving a notice to complete, excluding the day on which the notice is given. For this purpose, time is of the essence of the contract.

6.8.3 On receipt of a notice to complete:

(a) if the buyer paid no deposit, he is forthwith to pay a deposit of 10 per cent

(b) if the buyer paid a deposit of less than 10 per cent, he is forthwith to pay a further deposit equal to the balance of that 10 per cent.

7. REMEDIES

7.1 Errors and omissions

7.1.1 If any plan or statement in the contract, or in the negotiations leading to it, is or was misleading or inaccurate due to an error or omission, the remedies available are as follows.

7.1.2 When there is a material difference between the description or value of the property, or of any of the chattels included in the contract, as represented and as it is, the buyer is entitled to damages.

7.1.3 An error or omission only entitles the buyer to rescind the contract:

    (a) where it results from fraud or recklessness, or

    (b) where he would be obliged, to his prejudice, to accept property differing substantially (in quantity, quality or tenure) from what the error or omission had led him to expect.

7.2 Rescission

If either party rescinds the contract:

    (a) unless the rescission is a result of the buyer's breach of contract the deposit is to be repaid to the buyer with accrued interest

    (b) the buyer is to return any documents he received from the seller and is to cancel any registration of the contract.

7.3 Late completion

7.3.1 If there is default by either or both of the parties in performing their obligations under the contract and completion is delayed, the party whose total period of default is the greater is to pay compensation to the other party.

7.3.2 Compensation is calculated at the contract rate on an amount equal to the purchase price and the chattels price, less (where the buyer is the paying party) any deposit paid, for the period by which the paying party's default exceeds that of the receiving party, or, if shorter, the period between completion date and actual completion.

7.3.3 Any claim for loss resulting from delayed completion is to be reduced by any compensation paid under this contract.

7.3.4 Where the buyer holds the property as tenant of the seller and completion is defined, the seller may give notice to the buyer, before the date of actual completion, that he intends to take the net income from the property until completion. If he does so, he cannot claim compensation under condition 7.3.1 as well.

7.4 After completion

Completion does not cancel liability to perform any outstanding obligation under this contract.

7.5 Buyer's failure to comply with notice to complete

7.5.1 If the buyer fails to complete in accordance with a notice to complete, the following terms apply.

7.5.2 The seller may rescind the contract, and if he does so:
  (a) he may
    (i) forfeit and keep any deposit and accrued interest
    (ii) resell the property and any chattels included in the contract
    (iii) claim damages
  (b) the buyer is to return any documents he received from the seller and is to cancel any registration of the contract.

7.5.3 The seller retains his other rights and remedies.

7.6 Seller's failure to comply with notice to complete

7.6.1 If the seller fails to complete in accordance with a notice to complete, the following terms apply.

7.6.2 The buyer may rescind the contract, and if he does so:
  (a) the deposit is to be repaid to the buyer with accrued interest
  (b) the buyer is to return any documents he received from the seller and is, at the seller's expense, to cancel any registration of the contract.

7.6.3 The buyer retains his other rights and remedies.

8. LEASEHOLD PROPERTY

8.1 Existing leases

8.1.1 The following provisions apply to a sale of leasehold land.

8.1.2 The seller having provided the buyer with copies of the documents embodying the lease terms, the buyer is treated as entering into the contract knowing and fully accepting those terms.

8.1.3 The seller is to comply with any lease obligations requiring the tenant to insure the property.

8.2 New leases

8.2.1 The following provisions apply to a contract to grant a new lease.

8.2.2 The conditions apply so that: 'seller' means the proposed landlord 'buyer' means the proposed tenant 'purchase price' means the premium to be paid on the grant of a lease.

8.2.3 The lease is to be in the form of the draft attached to the contract.

8.2.4 If the term of the new lease will exceed seven years, the seller is to deduce a title which will enable the buyer to register the lease at HM Land Registry with an absolute title.

8.2.5 The seller is to engross the lease and a counterpart of it and is to send the counterpart to the buyer at least five working days before completion date.

8.2.6 The buyer is to execute the counterpart and deliver it to the seller on completion.

8.3 Consent

8.3.1 (a) The following provisions apply if a consent to let, assign or sub-let is required to complete the contract
  (b) In this condition 'consent' means consent in the form which satisfies the requirement to obtain it.

8.3.2 (a) The seller is to apply for the consent at his expense, and to use all reasonable efforts to obtain it

(b) The buyer is to provide all information and references reasonably required.

8.3.3 Unless he is in breach of his obligation under condition 8.3.2, either party may rescind the contract by notice to the other party if three working days before completion date (or before a later date on which the parties have agreed to complete the contract):

(a) the content has not been given, or

(b) the consent has been given subject to a condition to which a party reasonably objects.

In that case, neither party is to be treated as in breach of contract and condition 7.2 applies.

9. COMMONHOLD LAND

9.1 Terms used in this condition have the special meanings given to them in Part 1 of the Commonhold and Leasehold Reform Act 2002.

9.2 This condition applies to a disposition of commonhold land.

9.3 The seller having provided the buyer with copies of the current versions of the memorandum and articles of the commonhold association and of the commonhold community statement, the buyer is treated as entering into the contract knowing and fully accepting their terms.

9.4 If the contract is for the sale of property which is or includes part only of a commonhold unit:

(a) the seller is to apply for the written consent of the commonhold association at his expense and is to use all reasonable efforts to obtain it

(b) either the seller, unless he is in breach of his obligation under paragraph (a), or the buyer may rescind the contract by notice to the other party if three working days before completion date (or before a later date on which the parties have agreed to complete the contract) the consent has not been given. In that case, neither party is to be treated as in breach of contract and condition 7.2 applies.

10. CHATTELS

10.1 The following provisions apply to any chattels which are included in the contract, whether or not a separate price is to be paid for them.

10.2 The contract takes effect as a contract for sale of goods.

10.3 The buyer takes the chattels in the physical state they are in at the date of the contract.

10.4 Ownership of the chattels passes to the buyer on actual completion.

**Application to
change the register**

Land Registry

If you need more room than is provided for in a panel, use continuation sheet CS and attach to this form.

1.	**Administrative area and postcode** if known
2.	**Title number(s)**

3. If you have already made this application by **outline application**,
insert reference number:

4. **This application affects** *Place "X" in the appropriate box.*

☐ the **whole** of the title(s) *Go to panel 5.*

☐ **part** of the title(s) *Give a brief description of the property affected.*

---

5. **Application, priority and fees** *A fee calculator for all types of applications
can be found on Land Registry's website at www.landregistry.gov.uk/fees*

Nature of applications numbered   Value £   Fees paid £
in priority order
1.
2.
3.
                TOTAL £

Fee payment method: *Place "X" in the appropriate box.*
I wish to pay the appropriate fee payable under the current Land
Registration Fee Order:

☐ by cheque or postal order, amount £   made
payable to "Land Registry".

☐ by Direct Debit under an authorised agreement with Land
Registry.

FOR OFFICIAL USE ONLY
Record of fees paid

Particulars of under/over payments

Fees debited £

Reference number

---

6. **Documents lodged with this form** *Number the documents in sequence; copies should also be numbered and listed as separate
documents. Alternatively you may prefer to use Form DL. If you supply the original document and a certified copy, we shall assume that
you request the return of the original; if a certified copy is not supplied, we may retain the original document and it may be destroyed.*

---

7. **The applicant is:** *Please provide the full name(s) of the person(s) applying to change the register.*

The application has been lodged by:
Land Registry Key No. (if appropriate)
Name (if different from the applicant)
Address/DX No.

Reference
E-mail

Telephone No.	Fax No.

**FOR
OFFICIAL
USE ONLY
Codes
Dealing

Status**

8. Where you would like us to deal with someone else *We shall deal only with the applicant, or the person lodging the application if different, unless you place "X" against one or more of the statements below and give the necessary details.*

☐ Send title information document to the person shown below

☐ Raise any requisitions or queries with the person shown below

☐ Return original documents lodged with this form (see note in panel 6) to the person shown below
If this applies only to certain documents, please specify.

Name
Address/DX No.

Reference
E-mail

Telephone No.	Fax No.

9. Address(es) for service of the proprietor(s) of the registered estate(s). The address(es) will be entered in the register and used for correspondence and the service of notice. *Place "X" in the appropriate box(es). You may give up to three addresses for service one of which must be a postal address but does not have to be within the UK. The other addresses can be any combination of a postal address, a box number at a UK document exchange or an electronic address.*

☐ Enter the address(es) from the transfer/assent/lease

☐ Enter the address(es), including postcode, as follows:

☐ Retain the address(es) currently in the register for the title(s)

10. Disclosable overriding interests *Place "X" in the appropriate box.*

☐ This is not an application to register a registrable disposition or it is but no disclosable overriding interests affect the registered estate(s) *Section 27 of the Land Registration Act 2002 lists the registrable dispositions. Rule 57 of the Land Registration Rules 2003 sets out the disclosable overriding interests. Use Form DI to tell us about any disclosable overriding interests that affect the registered estate(s) identified in panel 2.*

☐ Form DI accompanies this application

The registrar may enter a notice of a disclosed interest in the register of title.

11. Information in respect of any new charge *Do not give this information if a Land Registry MD reference is printed on the charge, unless the charge has been transferred.*
Full name and address (including postcode) for service of notices and correspondence of the person to be registered as proprietor of each charge. *You may give up to three addresses for service one of which must be a postal address but does not have to be within the UK. The other addresses can be any combination of a postal address, a box number at a UK document exchange or an electronic address. For a company include company's registered number, if any. For Scottish companies use an SC prefix and for limited liability partnerships use an OC prefix before the registered number, if any. For foreign companies give territory in which incorporated.*

Unless otherwise arranged with Land Registry headquarters, we require a certified copy of the chargee's constitution (in English or Welsh) if it is a body corporate but is not a company registered in England and Wales or Scotland under the Companies Acts.

**12. Signature of applicant
or their conveyancer** _____ **Date** _____

Continuation sheet for use with application and disposition forms	Land Registry
	CS

1. Continued from Form   Title number(s)

2. *Before each continuation, state panel to be continued, e.g. "Panel 12 continued".*

Continuation sheet   of
*Insert sheet number and total number of
continuation sheets e.g. "sheet 1 of 3".*
© Crown copyright (ref: LR/HQ/CD-ROM) 6/03

Disclosable overriding interests   **Land Registry**

This form should be accompanied by either Form AP1 or Form FR1.

1.	Property

2.	Title number(s)

3. The applicant is: *Please provide the full name of the person applying to be registered as proprietor or to change the register.*	FOR OFFICIAL USE ONLY
The application has been lodged by: Land Registry Key No. (if appropriate) Name (if different from the applicant) Address/DX No.	Codes Dealing
Reference E-mail	Status
Telephone No. Fax No.	

4. In the panels below, please give details of any disclosable overriding interest that affects the estate to which the application relates.

Use panel 5 to tell us about any lease that is a disclosable overriding interest.

Use panel 6 to tell us about any other disclosable overriding interest. You may use as many Forms DI as necessary.

The registrar may enter notice of a disclosed interest in the register of title.

5. Please list below all unregistered disclosable leases in date order, starting with the oldest. You may use as many Forms DI as are necessary.

Please lodge a certified copy of either the original or the counterpart of each lease disclosed.

NB: If a previously noted lease has determined, the notice of it will only be cancelled on receipt of a Form CN1.

	Description of land leased	Date of Lease	Term and commencement date
e.g.	Flat 1, garage 3 and bin store	24.06.2002	5 years from 24.06.2002
a.			
b.			
c.			
d.			
e.			

6.	**Please list below any disclosable overriding interests which you have not included in panel 5**
a.	*Description of interest. For example, a legal easement.*

arising by virtue of _____

Deed or circumstances in which the interest arose.
[affects the land shown _____ on the enclosed plan].

b.	*Description of interest. For example, a legal easement.*

arising by virtue of _____

Deed or circumstances in which the interest arose.
[affects the land shown _____ on the enclosed plan].

c.	*Description of interest. For example, a legal easement.*

arising by virtue of _____

Deed or circumstances in which the interest arose.
[affects the land shown _____ on the enclosed plan].

© Crown copyright (ref: LR/HQ/CD-ROM) 6/03

List of documents
Please complete in duplicate.

Land Registry

DL

1. Property

2. Documents lodged

Notes (a) The first column is for official use only. If the Registry places an asterisk "*" in this column, it shows that we have kept that document.

(b) Number the documents in sequence; copies should also be numbered and listed as separate documents.

(c) If you supply the original document and a certified copy, we shall assume that you request the return of the original; if a certified copy is not supplied, we may retain the original document and it may be destroyed. For first registration applications, see the note in panel 6 of Form FR1.

OFFICIAL USE ONLY *(a)*	Item No. *(b)*	Date	Document *(c)*	Parties

OFFICIAL USE ONLY [a]	Item No. [b]	Date	Document [c]	Parties

**Cancellation of entries
relating to a
registered charge**

Land Registry

DS1

*This form should be accompanied by either Form AP1 or Form DS2.
If you need more room than is provided for in a panel, use continuation sheet CS and attach to this form.*

1. Title Number(s) of the Property
2. Property
3. Date
4. Date of charge
5. Lender
6. The Lender acknowledges that the property is no longer charged as security for the payment of sums due under the charge
7. Date of Land Registry facility letter, if any
8. *To be executed as a deed by the lender or in accordance with the above facility letter.*

© Crown copyright (ref: LR/HQ/CD-ROM) 6/03

**Application for official
copies of register/plan or
certificate in Form CI**

Land Registry **OC1**

Land Registry _____ Office

Use one form per title. If you need more room than is provided for in a panel, use continuation sheet CS and attach to this form.

1. **Administrative area** if known
2. **Title number** if known
3. **Property** Postal number or description
Name of road
Name of locality
Town
Postcode
Ordnance Survey map reference (if known)

4. **Payment of fee** *Place "X" in the appropriate box.*

☐ The Land Registry fee of £ [   ] accompanies this application.

☐ Debit the Credit Account mentioned in panel 5 with the appropriate fee payable under the current Land Registration Fee Order.

For official use only

Impression of fees

5. **The application has been lodged by:**
Land Registry Key No. (if appropriate)
Name
Address/DX No.

Reference
E-mail

Telephone No.	Fax No.

6. If the official copies are to be sent to anyone other than the applicant in panel 5, please supply the name and address of the person to whom they should be sent.

Reference

7. Where the title number is **not** quoted in panel 2, place "X" in the appropriate box(es). As regards this property, my application relates to:

☐ freehold estate   ☐ caution against first registration   ☐ franchise   ☐ manor
☐ leasehold estate   ☐ rentcharge   ☐ profit a prendre in gross

8. In case there is an application for registration pending against the title, place "X" in the appropriate box:

☐ I require an official copy back-dated to the day prior to the receipt of that application   **or**
☐ I require an official copy on completion of that application

9. **I apply for:** *Place "X" in the appropriate box(es) and indicate how many copies are required.*

☐ ___ official copy(ies) of the **register** of the above mentioned property
☐ ___ official copy(ies) of the **title plan or caution plan** of the above mentioned property

☐ ___ a certificate in Form CI, in which case **either**:

☐ an estate plan has been approved and the plot number is [   ]

or

☐ no estate plan has been approved and a certificate is to be issued in respect of the land shown _____ on the attached plan and copy

10. **Signature of applicant** _____ **Date** _____

Application by purchaser[a] for official search with priority of the whole of the land in a registered title or a pending first registration application

Land Registry **OS1**

Land Registry _____ Office

Use one form per title. If you need more room than is provided for in a panel, use continuation sheet CS and attach to this form.

1. Administrative area and postcode if known

2. Title number _Enter the title number of the registered estate or that allotted to the pending first registration._

3. Payment of fee [b] _Place "X" in the appropriate box._

☐ The Land Registry fee of £ [   ] accompanies this application.

☐ Debit the Credit Account mentioned in panel 4 with the appropriate fee payable under the current Land Registration Fee Order.

For official use only

Impression of fees

4. The application has been lodged by:[c]
Land Registry Key No. (if appropriate)
Name
Address/DX No.

Reference[d]
E-mail

Telephone No. | Fax No.

5. If the result of search is to be sent to anyone other than the applicant in panel 4, please supply the name and address of the person to whom it should be sent.

Reference[d]

6. Registered proprietor/Applicant for first registration _Enter FULL name(s) of the registered proprietor(s) of the registered estate in the above mentioned title **or** of the person(s) applying for first registration of the property specified in panel 10._

SURNAME/COMPANY NAME:

FORENAME(S):

SURNAME/COMPANY NAME:

FORENAME(S):

7. Search from date *For a search of a **registered title** enter in the box a date falling within the definition of search from date in rule 131 of the Land Registration Rules 2003.[c] If the date entered is not such a date the application may be rejected. In the case of a **pending first registration** search, enter the letters 'FR'.*

8. Applicant *Enter FULL name of each purchaser **or** lessee **or** chargee.*

9. Reason for application I certify that the applicant intends to: *Place "X" in the appropriate box.*

☐ | P | purchase   ☐ | C | take a registered charge

☐ | L | take a lease

10. Property details *Address or short description of the property.*

11. Type of search *Place "X" in the appropriate box.*

☐ **Registered land search**
Application is made to ascertain whether any adverse entry has been made in the register or day list since the date shown in panel 7.

☐ **Pending first registration search**
Application is made to ascertain whether any adverse entry has been made in the day list since the date of the pending first registration application referred to above.

12. Signature of applicant or their conveyancer _____ **Date** _____

Explanatory notes

(a) "Purchaser" is defined in Land Registration Rules 2003, r.131. In essence, it is a person who has entered, or intends to enter, into a disposition for valuable consideration as disponee where: (i) the disposition is a registrable disposition (see Land Registration Act 2002, s.27), or (ii) there is a person subject to a duty under the Land Registration Act 2002, s.6, to apply for registration, the application is pending and the disposition would have been a registrable disposition had the estate been registered.
An official search in respect of registered land made by a person other than a "purchaser" should be made in Form OS3.

(b) Cheques are payable to 'Land Registry'. If you hold a credit account but do not indicate that it should be debited, and do not enclose a cheque, the registrar may still debit your account.

(c) If you hold a credit account and want the official search certificate sent to an address different from that associated with your key number, enter your key number, reference and telephone number but otherwise leave panel 4 blank. Complete panel 5 instead.

(d) Enter a maximum of 25 characters including stops, strokes, punctuation etc.

(e) Enter the date shown as the subsisting entries date on an official copy of the register or given as the subsisting entries date at the time of an access by remote terminal.

Practice Guide 12 'Official Searches and Outline Applications' contains further information.

**Application for an
official search
of the index map**

Land Registry **SIM**

Land Registry_____ Office

If you need more room than is provided for in a panel, use continuation sheet CS and attach to this form.

1. **Administrative area**

2. Property to be searched
Postal number or description

Name of road
Name of locality
Town
Postcode
Ordnance Survey map reference (if known)
Known title number(s)

3. Payment of fee *Place "X" in the appropriate box.*

☐ The Land Registry fee of £ [   ] accompanies this application.

☐ Debit the Credit Account mentioned in panel 4 with the appropriate fee payable under the current Land Registration Fee Order.

For official use only
Impression of fees

4. The application has been lodged by:
Land Registry Key No. (if appropriate)
Name
Address/DX No.

Reference
E-mail

Telephone No.	Fax No.

5. If the result of search is to be sent to anyone other than the applicant in panel 4, please supply the name and address of the person to whom it should be sent.

Reference

6. **I apply for an official search of the index map in respect of the land referred to in panel 2 above and shown** _____ **on the attached plan.**

Any attached plan must contain sufficient details of the surrounding roads and other features to enable the land to be identified satisfactorily on the Ordnance Survey map. A plan may be unnecessary if the land can be identified by postal description.

7. Signature of applicant _____ **Date** _____

Explanatory notes

1. The purpose and scope of Official Searches of the Index Map are described in Practice Guide 10 'Official searches of the Index Map' obtainable from any Land Registry office. It can also be viewed online at www.landregistry.gov.uk.

2. Please send this application to the appropriate Land Registry office. This information is contained in Practice Guide 51 'Areas served by Land Registry offices'.

3. Please ensure that the appropriate fee payable under the current Land Registration Fee Order accompanies your application. If paying fees by cheque or postal order, these should be crossed and payable to "Land Registry". Where you have requested that the fee be paid by Credit Account, receipt of the certificate of result is confirmation that the appropriate fee has been debited.

© Crown copyright (ref: LR/HQ/Internet) 10/03

**Transfer of whole
of registered title(s)**

Land Registry

TR1

If you need more room than is provided for in a panel, use continuation sheet CS and attach to this form.

1.   Stamp Duty

Place "X" in the appropriate box or boxes and complete the appropriate certificate.

☐ It is certified that this instrument falls within category ☐ in the Schedule to the Stamp Duty (Exempt Instruments) Regulations 1987

☐ It is certified that the transaction effected does not form part of a larger transaction or of a series of transactions in respect of which the amount or value or the aggregate amount or value of the consideration exceeds the sum of   **£**

☐ It is certified that this is an instrument on which stamp duty is not chargeable by virtue of the provisions of section 92 of the Finance Act 2001

2.   Title Number(s) of the Property *Leave blank if not yet registered.*

3.   Property

4.   Date

5.   Transferor *Give full names and company's registered number if any.*

6.   Transferee for entry on the register *Give full name(s) and company's registered number, if any. For Scottish companies use an SC prefix and for limited liability partnerships use an OC prefix before the registered number, if any. For foreign companies give territory in which incorporated.*

Unless otherwise arranged with Land Registry headquarters, a certified copy of the Transferee's constitution (in English or Welsh) will be required if it is a body corporate but is not a company registered in England and Wales or Scotland under the Companies Acts.

7.   Transferee's intended address(es) for service (including postcode) for entry on the register *You may give up to three addresses for service one of which must be a postal address but does not have to be within the UK. The other addresses can be any combination of a postal address, a box number at a UK document exchange or an electronic address.*

8.   **The Transferor transfers the Property to the Transferee**

9.   Consideration *Place "X" in the appropriate box. State clearly the currency unit if other than sterling. If none of the boxes applies, insert an appropriate memorandum in the additional provisions panel.*

☐ The Transferor has received from the Transferee for the Property the sum of *In words and figures.*

☐ *Insert other receipt as appropriate.*

☐ The transfer is not for money or anything which has a monetary value

10. The Transferor transfers with *Place "X" in the appropriate box and add any modifications.*

☐ full title guarantee   ☐ limited title guarantee

---

11. Declaration of trust *Where there is more than one Transferee, place "X" in the appropriate box.*

☐ The Transferees are to hold the Property on trust for themselves as joint tenants

☐ The Transferees are to hold the Property on trust for themselves as tenants in common in equal shares

☐ The Transferees are to hold the Property *Complete as necessary.*

---

12. Additional provisions *Insert here any required or permitted statements, certificates or applications and any agreed covenants, declarations, etc.*

---

13. Execution *The Transferor must execute this transfer as a deed using the space below. If there is more than one Transferor, all must execute. Forms of execution are given in Schedule 9 to the Land Registration Rules 2003. If the transfer contains Transferee's covenants or declarations or contains an application by the Transferee (e.g. for a restriction), it must also be executed by the Transferee (all of them, if there is more than one).*

Glossary

If you are doing your own conveyancing there are certain terms you may come across that you need to be able to understand.

agreement See *contract*

attorney See *power of attorney*

banker's draft A cheque drawn by a bank on its own funds, rather than being drawn by an individual on his or her own account. It is generally regarded as being as good as cash. The bank will take the money from your account before giving you a draft and will charge a fee for the service. Although it is as good as cash in that it will not 'bounce', it is not technically 'cleared funds', that is credited to your account, and you will still have to wait the usual length of time for the money to be transferred from the paying bank into your account. You cannot, therefore, draw against it until it has cleared without obtaining prior agreement from your bank.

Charge Certificate See *Land Certificate*

Charges Register One of the three registers maintained by Land Registry for a property. It records interests adverse to the owner (see also *Property Register* and *Proprietorship Register*).

chattels The contents of the house, e.g. carpets, curtains and furniture etc., which would not pass to the buyer of the house. However, it is sometimes difficult to determine whether some items, for example curtain rails and TV aerials, fixed to the structure of the house, are part of the house or not and so the *Fixtures, Fittings and Contents Form* should be completed to clarify what is and what is not included in the sale.

completion This is the day in the conveyancing process on which the buyer hands over the balance of the purchase price (that is, the agreed price less the deposit already paid) and in return is entitled to receive the keys to the house. The seller must move out and give vacant possession to the buyer.

completion information and requisitions on title form A form used by buyers to enquire about the arrangements for completion.

contract (or agreement) The document which sets out the terms of the 'deal' between the buyer and seller. As well as containing details of the sale – who is selling what to whom and at what price – it also contains small print laying down the rights and obligations of the buyer and seller, for example what will happen if the buyer refuses to go through with the purchase. This small print will usually consist of the *Standard Conditions of Sale* (see below).

contract race The situation where a seller sends draft contracts to two or more prospective buyers and offers to exchange contracts with the buyer who is able to proceed first. If you enter into a contract race you risk spending large sums on searches and surveys, only to find that someone else buys the house. Avoid this if at all possible.

conveyancer Solicitors and others (e.g. licensed conveyancers) who are permitted by law to carry out conveyancing work in return for a fee.

conveyancing The legal and administrative process involved in transferring the ownership of land or any buildings on it from one owner to another.

covenant This is an agreement to do or not to do something that is contained in a deed. In certain circumstances, a buyer of land will be bound by covenants entered into by previous owners of the land. Covenants to repair boundary fences or not to use land in a particular way are very common.

deed This is a document which is signed in a special way. All transfers of the ownership of land must be by deed to be valid. To constitute a deed, a document must indicate that it is intended to be a deed (for example, it must be headed 'This Deed', or it is stated to be 'Signed as a Deed') and the signatures of the parties need to be witnessed, with the witness also signing.

deposit Under the terms of the contract, the seller is entitled to insist upon the buyer paying part of the purchase price on exchange of contracts. Traditionally this is 10 per cent of the price, but often a lower figure can be negotiated. The deposit is a sign of the buyer's good faith and intention to go through with the purchase. Should the buyer refuse to proceed without any good cause, the seller is entitled to keep the deposit, whether or not he or she actually suffers any loss due to the buyer withdrawing. It is unwise for a seller to enter into a sale contract without receiving a deposit.

development Planning permission from the local planning authority (usually the district or unitary council) is usually required before any development can be carried out on land. Development includes any material change in use or any building work. You should not buy property which breaches the planning laws as you could also be liable for penalties if you continue an existing breach.

easement This is a right to use land owned by someone else in a particular way. Common easements include a right of way, such as a right to walk/drive a car over someone else's land; a right of drainage, that is a right for your drainage pipes to pass through someone else's land; and a right of light, a right for the light to your windows to pass over someone else's land. If you buy land that is affected by an easement, you will be bound to allow that right to continue without interruption.

engross; engrossment An old-fashioned term referring to the preparation of a fresh copy of a document (the engrossment), which will then be signed by all parties to the transaction. Engrossments are prepared mainly when the original draft document has been so heavily amended that it cannot be used.

Enquiries before Contract See *Property Information Form*

exchange of contracts This is the moment when the contract becomes binding on the buyer and seller. Until exchange, either party is free to withdraw from the transaction without penalty. Two copies of the contract are prepared; the buyer signs one and the seller the other. The two are then simply swapped over (exchanged), the buyer sending his or her signed copy to the seller and vice versa. It is usual for the buyer to pay the seller a deposit on exchange (see above).

execution The signing and witnessing of a deed, such as the Transfer (see below).

Fee simple See *freehold*

Fixtures, Fittings and Contents Form A list of the items in the house indicating which are to be taken by the seller and which are to be left behind and purchased by the buyer. It is completed by the seller and handed over to the buyer at the outset of the transaction.

freehold Property held absolutely (that is, until the end of time). Also known as 'fee simple'.

indemnity covenant A clause in the Transfer in which the buyer undertakes to indemnify (i.e., compensate) the seller in respect of any future breaches in any of the restrictions in the title deeds that affect the property.

intestate; intestacy A person dies intestate if there is no valid will. The deceased's property will then pass according to a set of rules laid down by statute. Depending upon the size of the estate, this may be to the surviving spouse or to the spouse and children.

joint tenancy One of the two ways in which co-owners may own land. On the death of one co-owner, that person's interest passes automatically to the survivor(s); it cannot be disposed of by will. However, while they are alive, any co-owner can convert their interest into that of a tenant in common (see below) – this is known as 'severing' the joint tenancy.

Land Certificate A document formerly issued by Land Registry containing details of the ownership of the land. If there was a mortgage on the land, a Charge Certificate was issued instead; this contained the same details of ownership, together with the deed creating the mortgage. It used to be necessary for the Land or Charge Certificate to be handed over to the buyer on completion. However, as from 13 October 2003, this is no longer necessary, although it will often still happen. Note that a Land or Charge Certificate should not be accepted as evidence of ownership of the land, as it may be out of date. Official Copy Entries, that is, copies of the Register made by Land Registry, are used as proof of ownership (see below).

Land Registry A public body which keeps records of the ownership of land in England and Wales. It is organised on a district basis. Land Registry Offices are located throughout the country, each being responsible for the records for its own designated area (see Appendix I).

Law Society The body charged with overseeing the solicitors' profession in England and Wales. The Society lays down and enforces standards of professional conduct, for example compliance with undertakings (see below).

leasehold Ownership of property for a fixed number of years granted by a lease which sets out the obligations of the lessee (or tenant), for example regarding payment of rent to the landlord, repairs and insurance; as opposed to freehold property, where ownership is absolute.

local (authority) search A list of questions requesting information about the property which might be contained in the local authority's records.

mortgage A transaction which gives a lender extensive rights over your land in return for the loan. You cannot sell the land without paying off the loan, and if you do not keep up with the repayments, the lender is entitled to evict you from the house and then sell it without your consent in order to recover the amount owing. The borrower will be entitled to any of the sale proceeds left over after paying off the mortgage debt and the costs of the sale. When buying a house you must ensure that any existing mortgages are discharged (paid off) on completion.

mortgagee The lender under a mortgage, i.e., a bank or building society.

mortgagor The borrower under a mortgage, i.e., the landowner.

Official Copy Entries Copies of the entries at Land Registry relating to the house. These are proof of the ownership of the house.

personal representatives Persons authorised by the court to deal with a deceased's property. They may be either executors (if nominated by the deceased in his or her will) or administrators (if there was no nomination by will). Executors are authorised to act by the court under a grant of probate; administrators under a grant of letters of administration.

planning permission; planning consent The permission required from the local authority before any development can take place on land.

power of attorney A formal deed drawn up to enable someone (the attorney) to act on your behalf and in particular to sign deeds on your behalf. If a seller is selling through an attorney, you will need professional advice to ensure that the sale is authorised.

pre-contract package This is an 'information pack' about the property to be sold; it is prepared by the seller and sent to the buyer at the outset of the transaction.

Preliminary Enquiries Form See *Property Information Form*

probate The formal process of obtaining a court order authorising the administration of the estate of a deceased person. See *personal representatives*.

Property Information Form (PIF) This is a list of questions relating to the property to be sold. It is completed by the seller and handed over to the buyer at the outset of the transaction. Also known as a Preliminary Enquiries Form or an Enquiries before Contract Form.

Property Register One of the three parts of a Land or Charge Certificate. It describes the property and rights that go with it.

Proprietorship Register Another of the parts of a Land or Charge Certificate. It records the names of the owners and any restrictions on their right to sell.

purchase deed See *Transfer*

redemption figure The amount required to 'redeem', or pay off, a mortgage.

Registered Charge The name given to a mortgage of registered land.

requisitions on title The questions asked about the seller's title to land, and the matters raised before completion.

restrictive covenant This is an agreement restricting or limiting in some way the use of a piece of land. An agreement to 'use only as a single private dwellinghouse' is a common form of restrictive covenant affecting houses. Even though this agreement was entered into by a previous owner of the land, a buyer will also be bound by it if the covenant is registered at Land Registry.

severing a joint tenancy The process of converting a joint tenancy into a tenancy in common. This can be done in several ways, including the service of a notice in writing on the other joint tenant(s).

stamp duty land tax A government tax payable by buyers of property. Previously called stamp duty. It was so called because a 'stamp' was embossed on the Transfer to show that the tax had been paid. It is now payable on completion of a new form of tax return called a Land Transaction Return in Form SDLT 1. The duty varies according to the value of the house; houses valued at £60,000 or under are exempt from duty.

Standard Conditions of Sale A standard set of terms and conditions which are incorporated within conveyancing contracts. The conditions were devised by the Law Society and strive to set a fair balance between the rights and obligations of both the buyer and the seller. They are used in virtually all residential conveyancing transactions. A copy of the Conditions is set out in Appendix II.

'subject to contract' This form of words prefixing a letter is designed to ensure that the letter cannot be used as evidence of a written contract. It is strictly unnecessary, but is still used from time to time.

tenancy in common One of the two ways in which co-owners can own land. On the death of a tenant in common, the deceased's interest in the land will pass by will or intestacy in the usual way (see also *joint tenancy*).

title deeds The documents conferring and evidencing ownership of land. In registered land there are no title deeds, the register being the only proof of ownership necessary.

Title information document A document issued by Land Registry on completion of registration of a buyer. It contains copies of the new entries on the register, but it is not proof of title and does not need to be produced in connection with a subsequent sale.

title number The unique number allocated to each property by Land Registry. You will need to refer to your title number in any correspondence with Land Registry.

Transfer The document which passes the ownership of the house from the seller to the buyer. Sometimes called the *purchase deed*. It must be in the prescribed form laid down by Land Registry.

trust An arrangement under which the owner of property (the trustee) is obliged to hold that property for the sole benefit of another (the beneficiary).

undertaking A promise given by a solicitor or licensed conveyancer (whether verbally or in writing) in the course of a transaction. It is binding upon the solicitor and if not complied with may result in disciplinary proceedings being brought against the solicitor by the Law Society and against licensed conveyancers by the Council for Licensed Conveyancers.

vacant possession This term is usually included in all contracts for the sale of residential property. It means that on completion the seller must hand over the house to the buyer in an empty condition, that is without anyone being in occupation and without any furniture or other items (such as rubbish) preventing the buyer from moving in.

will A formal document which sets out who is to inherit a person's property on death.

Addresses

(For the addresses of the various District Land Registries, see Appendix I)

Building guarantees

National House Building Council (NHBC)
Buildmark House
Chiltern Avenue
Amersham
Buckinghamshire HP6 5AP
Tel: (01494) 735363
Website: www.nhbc.co.uk

Forms

Oyez Straker Group
Oyez offers a postal, telephone and online service for the forms you will need. To order by telephone call (0870) 737 7370 to order and purchase forms by credit card. Alternatively, order online at www.oyezformslink.co.uk

The Stationery Office Ltd
The Stationery Office offers an online and telephone ordering service for some of the forms you may require. To order by telephone call (0870) 600 5522, or visit the website at www.tsonline.co.uk

Stationery Office bookshops

Birmingham
68–69 Bull Street
Birmingham B4 6AD
Tel: 0121-236 9696

Cardiff
18–19 High Street
Cardiff CF10 1PT
Tel: 029-2039 5548

London
123 Kingsway
London WC2B 6PQ
Tel: 020-7242 6393

Manchester
9–21 Princess Street
Albert Square
Manchester M60 8AS
Tel: 0161-834 7201

Legal matters

Consumer Complaints Service (formerly known as the Office for the Supervision of Solicitors)
Victoria Court
8 Dormer Place
Leamington Spa
Warwickshire CV32 5AE
Tel: (01926) 820082
Helpline: (0845) 608 6565
Website: www.lawsociety.org.uk

Council for Licensed Conveyancers
16 Glebe Road
Chelmsford
Essex CM1 1QG
Tel: (01245) 349599
Website: www.conveyancer.org.uk

The Law Society
113 Chancery Lane
London WC2A 1PL
Tel: 020-7242 1222
Website: www.lawsociety.org.uk

Publications

Which? Books
Castlemead
Gascoyne Way
Hertford SG14 1LH
Freephone: (0800) 252100

Searches

All searches
Jordans Ltd
21 St Thomas Street
Bristol BS1 6JS
Tel: 0117-918 1498
Website: www.jordans.co.uk
Jordans will make all searches on your behalf – for a fee – without the need to buy the forms

Bankruptcy searches
Land Registry
Land Charges Department
Plumer House
Tailyour Road
Crownhill
Plymouth PL6 5HY
Tel: (01752) 636666
Website: www.landreg.gov.uk

Brine (salt-mining) searches
Cheshire Brine Subsidence Compensation Board
80 Lower Bridge Street
Chester CH1 1SW
Tel: (01244) 602576

China Clay mining
English China Clays plc/Imerys
John Keay House
St Austell
Cornwall PL25 4DJ
Tel: (01726) 74482
Website: www.imerys.com

Coal-mining searches
The Coal Authority
200 Lichfield Lane
Berry Hill
Mansfield
Nottinghamshire NG18 4RG
Tel: (01623) 427162
Recorded information on procedure and fees: (0845) 601 2608
Helpline: (0845) 762648
Website: www.coal.gov.uk

Environmental searches
Landmark Information Group
67 Abbey Court
Eagle Way
Sowton Industrial Estate
Exeter EX2 7HY
Tel: (01392) 441700
Website: www.landmark-information.co.uk

Jordans Ltd
21 St Thomas Street
Bristol BS1 6JS
Tel: 0117-918 1498
Website: www.jordans.co.uk

Tin-mining searches
Cornwall Consultants
Parc Vean House
Coach Lane
Redruth
Cornwall TR15 2TT
Tel: (01209) 313511
Website:
www.cornwallconsultants.co.uk

Waterways and canals
The Environment Agency
Rio House
Waterside Drive
Aztec West
Almondsbury BS32 4UD
Tel: (01454) 624400
Website:
www.environment-agency.gov.uk

Stamp duty land tax

This can no longer be paid at a local
Stamp Office and can be paid only
by post to:

Inland Revenue (Stamp Taxes/SDLT)
Comben House
Farriers Way
Netherton L30 4RN

The Land Transaction Return can be
completed online at
www.ir-online.gov.uk/stamps/

Stamps Office
If you need help with any part of the
return or with anything in the
guidance notes, phone the Stamp
Taxes enquiry line on (0845) 603 0135

Payments Office
If you need help with payments,
phone the Payments Office enquiry
line on (01274) 530750
Forms Orderline
If you need to order new payment
books, forms or guidance contact the
Forms Orderline on (0845) 302 1472

Inland Revenue Online Services
Helpdesk
For help and advice on any technical
issues to do with registering and
accessing this service, email
helpdesk@ir-efile.gov.uk, or phone
(0845) 605 5999

Inland Revenue:
www.inlandrevenue.gov.uk/home.htm

Index